GUITARS

SOUNDS, CHROME & STARS

Publishers Note

Though not a strict chronology, the structure of this book has been inspired by
the evolution of the guitar as an instrument, in general terms, and by the historical
influence of individual makers on each other.

Publisher and Creative Director: Nick Wells
Art Director: Mike Spender
Picture Research: Victoria Lyle and Gemma Walters
Commissioning Editor: Christine Kidney
Digital Design and Production: Chris Herbert
Layout Design: Dave Jones and Mike Spender

With thanks to: Chelsea Edwards, Amanda Fitzgerald,
Beverley Jollands and Sara Robson

First published 2007 by
FLAME TREE PUBLISHING
Crabtree Hall, Crabtree Lane
Fulham, London SW6 6TY
United Kingdom

www.flametreepublishing.com

Flame Tree is part of The Foundry Creative Media Company Limited

A copy of the CIP data for this book is available from the British Library.

ISBN: 978 1 84451 972 9

Picture Credits

Brook Guitars: 31; Carl Tremblay: photographs originally published in *Dangerous Curves:
The Art of the Guitar*. Published in 2000 by MFA Publications, a division of the Museum
of Fine Arts, Boston: 3, 5, 7 (l), 72–73, 90–91, 115, 142–43, 150; Epiphone Guitars: 70;
Foundry Arts: 81, 83; Fylde Guitars: 30; Gibson Guitars: 58, 103, 104–05, 109; Hauser
Guitars: 36–37; Maxo / Wikimedia: 71; C.F. Martin & Co.: 12, 14; Optek Fretlight: 197;
Parker Guitars: 140–41; Paul Reed Smith Guitars: 152, 154–55, 156–57; Shuttershock:
1, 4 (l), 5 (l), 6, 7 (r), 8, 10–11, 20–21, 29, 35, 48, 49, 54–55, 66, 95, 102, 106–07,
108–09, 110–11, 114, 116–17, 123, 124–25, 126, 127, 128–29, 130, 132–33,
136–37, 146–47, 148, 149, 153, 176, 182, 200; Steve Hackett: 9; Taylor Guitars: 93;
vintageguitar.co.uk: 32, 33. All other images courtesy of DK Images.

Acknowledgements

With thanks to Andy's Guitars and to Mick Jackson, editor of the *Guitarist* magazine, for his generous advice.

Printed in China

GUITARS
SOUNDS, CHROME & STARS

GRAHAM KEMPSTER

FOREWORD BY STEVE HACKETT

**FLAME TREE
PUBLISHING**

CONTENTS

THE SEMI-ACOUSTIC GUITAR 54

THE ACOUSTIC FLAT TOP:
MODERN BRITISH LUTHIERS

THE CLASSICAL AND FLAMENCO GUITAR

THE ACOUSTIC ARCHTOP

RESONATORS

THE ELECTRO ACOUSTIC GUITAR

THE ELECTRIC GUITAR 94

THE TWIN-NECK ELECTRIC GUITAR

THE BASS GUITAR

DIGITAL, SYNTHESIZER & MIDI GUITARS 190

FOREWORD

Forty-five years ago I started out wrestling with my first guitar ... a beast that had such a brutally high action that it would take the strength of a team of horses to hold down virtually any chord. I assumed my lacerated fingers would get better – surely it was just the price, or rather the induction into that select club of incredibly strong and impossibly handsome young guys who literally had the world at their fingertips. After two months the mythical "calluses" had failed to appear. My fingertips were still bloodied stumps. What was I to do? I loved the sound of the guitar but gritted my teeth every time I was about to attempt once more to waltz through what felt like wire. I was a poor, misguided wretch and a self-taught one at that.

Then one glorious day some six months later a school friend bought a guitar that cost him all of six quid from the local Army and Navy store near London's Victoria Station. A kindly shop assistant had advised him to buy a nylon-strung instrument which was (I thought over time) plainly more use to me than him. The action seemed so gracefully low and the touch of the strings felt more like silk than the usual rusted metal fibre of my own instrument. So I fell in love with the sound of those silken caresses and have remained so ever since. Please don't get me wrong, I'm not extolling the virtues of nylon versus metal strings. When you get the tension right for your own style and taste, everything gets a little easier. Light gauge metal strings can feel as slack as rubber bands to a heavy handed player who is more comfortable imagining himself chipping wood with the "right" axe. Then there's the player who wants to hit each string very lightly and glide over single note phrases ... at least that's the theory anyway. Guitar players aren't gods, they're ordinary blokes (and blokesses) like you and me who sometimes manage to surprise themselves. We all make mistakes, especially when we're trying for the moon.

So forgive yourself everytime you fluff a tricky manoeuvre, it's all part of the game and remember that there's no joy comparable to being able to manage to play those first three chords. It might be C, F, G or A, D, E but armed with these three chords you can play along with or even write, literally, thousands of songs.

Did I forget to mention why the guitar is currently the world's most popular instrument? It's the following: the range of sounds that can be drawn from different guitars is virtually limitless. So take a look inside these pages at some of the finest ideas guitar manufacturers have ever had since the dawn of time and let's doff our caps to those geniuses who have made a life a lot more interesting for a world full of guitar addicts such as my humble self.

STEVE HACKETT

THE ACOUSTIC GUITAR

Instruments similar to the guitar have been popular for at least 5,000 years. Guitar-like instruments appear in ancient carvings and statues from the old Iranian capital of Susa. The Vinaccia family of mandolin luthiers may have built the earliest known six-string guitar: Gaetano Vinaccia's signature is on the label of a six-stringed instrument, made in Naples in 1779. Modern dimensions of the classical guitar were established by Antonio de Torres, working in Seville in the 1850s. He was able to demonstrate the superiority of fan strutting over transverse table bracing, leading to greater resonance and better distribution of sound across the board. With Torres, the guitar took another step up the evolutionary ladder. It was now larger, more robust and with a fuller tone. A number of the creators of the modern American instrument were first or second generation émigrés from Europe. Orville Gibson was born of English parents in New York, Epiphone was founded by the Greek instrument maker, Anastasios Stathopoulo, but the first and most influential of all the Europeans was German luthier, C.F. Martin, who settled in New York in 1833. With such innovations as X bracing, the introduction of the 14-fret neck and the design of the Dreadnought, Martin instruments have been the most copied of all acoustic guitars.

THE ACOUSTIC FLAT TOP

Martin

For well over 150 years The Martin Guitar Company has been continuously producing instruments that are acknowledged to be some of the finest in the world. The 1850s marked one of C. F. Martin's major design innovations, the X bracing system for the guitar top. Still in use today on all Martin steel-string models, the bracing system is largely responsible for the distinctive Martin tone, characterized by the brilliant treble and powerful bass response. The X bracing, Martin's designs for the shape of the guitar body and the use of decorative inlay work have influenced almost every maker of acoustic guitars, both directly and indirectly. Martin's straightforward model-number system has a number or letter before the hyphen that relates to the size of the body. From smallest to largest they include, 2, 1, 0, 00, 000, OM, D. The number following the hyphen refers to the body ornamentation, the higher the number the more decorative the finish, for example 18, 28, 35, 45.

Martin 1902 00-45S

One of Martin's early 12-fret models, reissued as a special edition. This gorgeous small-bodied guitar has a solid Adirondack spruce top, solid Brazilian rosewood back and sides, with 42-style top and side inlay of abalone pearl, slotted headstock with solid Brazilian rosewood and flowerpot abalone pearl inlay. The fingerboard is solid ebony with a scale length of 25 in (63.2 cm) in with inlays of Tree Of Life select pearl. A tortoise-colour pickguard is inlaid with abalone. C. F. Martin IV signs each one of these guitars.

Martin 00-18

Introduced in 1898, the 00-18 featured an unbound ebony fingerboard, rosewood back and sides and a rectangle bridge. In 1902 small dot fingerboard markers were used at the 5th, 7th and 9th frets, soundhole inlay of nine alternating black and white rings, in between two single black rings, and a black back stripe. 1917 saw the introduction of mahogany back and sides. A tortoiseshell pickguard, five-ply top binding and graduated dot fingerboard inlays from the 5th to the 15th fret were added in 1932. Other changes included a rosewood fingerboard (1940), body binding to black (1966) and a black pickguard (1967). The current model is the Martin 00-18V, with a specification that includes: sitka spruce top, mahogany back and sides, ebony fingerboard, and Gotoh open-geared tuning machines with 'butterbean' knobs.

Martin 000-28

At the turn of the twentieth century, Martin had been experimenting with bigger bodies to increase the sound and projection of their guitars. At that time the widest body was size 00 at 14 in (35.9 cm). In 1902 the company introduced the 15 in (38.1 cm) 000, made to compete with mandolins and banjos and, although slow to start, sales grew steadily throughout the 1920s. Martin's current catalogue lists the 000-28 with sitka spruce top, East Indian rosewood back, sides and headplate and ebony fingerboard.

Martin OM-28

The 'Orchestra Model' came about in 1929, due to Perry Bechtel, who was a virtuoso plectrum banjo player. He wanted Martin to make him a guitar to which he could easily adapt his banjo style. Martin began with a 000 size guitar and squared the body's shoulders to allow a re-shaped neck which joined at the 14th fret instead of the 12th fret of earlier guitars. It was later named the OM-28 and was the first Martin specifically designed for steel strings. This was the start of the modern flat-top guitar, and proved so popular that it was copied by other guitar manufacturers and became the industry standard.

Martin D-18

Possibly the most famous and copied of Martin's guitars, the Dreadnought series was named after the huge British battleships of the First World War. The D-1 (mahogany) and D-2 (rosewood) were originally made for the Ditson company of Boston from 1916, who sold the instruments under their own name exclusively through their stores. When Ditson's went out of business in the late 1920s, the Martin company re-designed and improved the guitar and in 1934 began producing Dreadnoughts that carried the Martin name. The earlier D-1 became the D-18, and the D-2 became the D-28, both with a neck that joined at the 14th fret. The D-18 and D-28 soon became the favourite among country and bluegrass players, who needed a massive sound to compete with fiddlers and banjoists. Spruce top, mahogany back and sides and rosewood fingerboard.

Martin D-28

The D-28 has a spruce top and rosewood body, and more decoration than the D-18. This Martin guitar has been the mainstream of the Martin line since its introduction. Sitka spruce top with black/white binding, East Indian rosewood back, sides and headplate and ebony fingerboard. The body is

Martin D-45

The D-45 was first made in 1933 for 'singing cowboy' star Gene Autry, who wanted an ultra-fancy instrument with intricate abalone trim, and his name in pearl script along the fingerboard. The Martin D-45 was built between 1938 and 1942 but discontinued until 1968, since when it has been in constant production. It is the most desirable of all acoustic flat-top guitars. The Dreadnought style has become the benchmark for flat-top guitar design, and currently accounts for some eighty per cent of Martin's yearly production.

Gibson L-1

The Gibson L-1 was first introduced in 1902 as an archtop guitar. It had a single-bound top and neck, bound soundhole, ebony fingerboard with dot inlays and mahogany back and sides. In 1926 Gibson discontinued the archtop and reintroduced the L-1 as a flat top, selling for about $50. The first versions were made with maple back and sides, 25 in (63.5 cm) scale length, three rings around the soundhole and a brown finish. From 1927 on the L-1 was made from mahogany, with one ring around the soundhole and a sunburst finish. The Gibson L-1 was famously used by the great bluesman Robert Johnson.

Gibson SJ-200

With a background in making archtop guitars, it took some time for Gibson to approach Martin's level of commitment to the flat top. The 'Super Jumbo' range evolved from a collaboration with one of Hollywood's earliest singing cowboys, Ray Whitley, who suggested a number of ideas to increase the guitar's bass response. The instrument appeared in the stores in 1938 and was named, like other Gibsons, after its price: $200. Gibson used rosewood for the back and sides on the early models but changed to maple after the Second World War. The necks are maple with an ebony fretboard and pearl fingerboard inlays. With its nine-ply binding, pearl-inlaid 'mustache' bridge and elaborate pickguard decorated with flowers and vines, the SJ-200 was, according to Gibson literature, 'the King of the flat-top guitars'.

Gibson Country Western

Introduced in 1956 as a natural-finish version of the Gibson Southern Jumbo, the guitar featured a spruce top with mahogany back and sides and a rosewood fingerboard with Gibson's distinctive 'double parallelogram' inlays. From 1956 to 1962 the Country Western had round shoulders; from mid 1962 square shoulders and the three-point pickguard were introduced and the model was renamed the SJN Country Western. The specification remained basically unchanged until production ceased in 1978.

Gibson Hummingbird

The Hummingbird guitar was Gibson's first square-shouldered dreadnought. Although fairly expensive when introduced in 1960, it was an immediate success, thanks to its playability and rich tone. It had a mahogany back and sides, gold tuners, double parallelogram fingerboard inlays, an elaborate hummingbird design on the pickguard, and came in a cherry sunburst finish. From 1960 to the present there have been no significant changes to this model.

Gibson J-45

A real workhorse of a guitar, and probably Gibson's most popular acoustic ever made, the J-45 replaced the J-35 in 1942. It had a spruce top, mahogany back and sides, white/black/white binding, 19 fret fingerboard and a banner on the headstock which read: 'Only a Gibson is good enough.' The J-45 became a huge success due to its big sound, warm, fat tone, Gibson-build quality, and the fact that it was not that expensive to buy. In 1946 the 'Only a Gibson' banner was dropped and a belly bridge was added. 1950 saw the introduction of the 20-fret fingerboard. In 1969 the J-45 was made with a square-shouldered body and black teardrop pickguards. They were discontinued in 1982. 1984 saw the reintroduction of the original model of the J-45 with round shoulders, tortoiseshell pickguard, unbound rosewood fingerboard and dot inlays.

Gibson Dove

In 1962 Gibson introduced the Dove as their number two guitar below the J-200, with a sound very similar to the Hummingbird. It had a spruce top with matched maple back and sides, a three-piece maple neck, 20-fret rosewood or ebony fingerboard, and a beautiful dove inlaid pickguard. These guitars were available in cherry or sunburst finishes. The Dove became extremely popular after Elvis Presley used one on tour during 1976–77.

Epiphone Texan

After Gibson's purchase of the company in 1957, Gibson made all Epiphones until the late 1960s and made flat tops introduced in 1958. The Texan (model number FT-79) had a round-shouldered body shape, mahogany back and sides, angled-side rectangle fingerboard inlays, slashed C logo on pickguard and plastic tuner buttons. In 1962 an adjustable saddle bridge was added, and in 1969 metal tuner buttons and a square-shouldered body were the last changes to the specification until the model was discontinued in 1970. Paul McCartney acquired an Epiphone Texan in 1964, which, according to the manufacturer, had a list price at that time of $175. This guitar can be heard on a number of mid-period Beatles recordings, and McCartney composed and recorded 'Yesterday' with the Texan in 1965.

Epiphone Broadway

Introduced in 1931 as part of Epiphone's 'Masterbilt' series, the Epiphone was cheaper than the Deluxe and Emperor models. It featured a 16 3/8-in (41.6-cm) wide body, 25 1/2 in (64.8 cm) scale, walnut back and sides, three-ply binding on top and back, single-bound ebony fingerboard, and bound Masterbilt peghead with flowers. Changes to the Broadway over the years included: in 1934 gold-plated parts and wandering vine peghead inlay; in 1939 frequensator tailpiece, maple back and sides; in 1941 a natural finish was available; in 1951 it gained a fat column peghead inlay; and in 1958 Gibson made an electric cutaway with two New York pickups. The acoustic model was discontinued.

Following Maccaferri's departure, Selmer introduced the famous Modele Jazz, which incorporated an oval-shaped soundhole, a cutaway at the 15th fret and a radiused ebony fingerboard extending over the soundhole, providing a 24th fret under the high E string. Django used this model until his death.

THE ACOUSTIC FLAT TOP: MODERN NORTH-AMERICAN LUTHIERS

Santa Cruz Tony Rice Model

Richard Hoover began building guitars and mandolins in 1972. By 1976 his focus was on the modern steel-string guitar, and along with two partners, he set up the Santa Cruz Guitar Company in California. Each guitar receives complete, individual attention due to the 'bench style' of building, meaning that each craftsman can concentrate on his own speciality, and also review the work of those who have completed stages before him. More than half of the Santa Cruz output is custom-built. All guitar tops are graduated and tuned by hand, ensuring a high level of consistency and sound within each model line, as well as the ability for custom voicing. The Tony Rice Model came about after the bluegrass guitarist wanted a guitar based on his legendary 1930s Martin D-28, once owned by Clarence White. This instrument has a 15-in (38.1-cm) body, a top of sitka spruce, and Indian rosewood back, sides and neck. The edges and soundhole are trimmed with herringbone inlays and the 'Santa Cruz' logo is inset at the 12th fret.

Collings D3

In the opinion of many guitar aficionados, Collings guitars are the standard of comparison in both styling and construction, harking back to the legendary Martin guitars of the 1930s. Bill Collings makes his guitars in Austin, Texas. The D3 is Collings' top-of-the-line dreadnought with a spruce top, rosewood back and sides, ivoroid bindings and mahogany neck.

Olson SJ Small Jumbo

James A. Olson has been handcrafting guitars since 1977. His instruments began getting attention in the mid 1980s, after Phil Keaggy commissioned the first cedar-topped SJ guitar. James Taylor purchased three Olsons and, through Taylor's visibility, Olson guitars became prized around the world. The SJ is one of the best-selling Olson instruments. It comes with rosewood back and sides, capped with a top of cedar. The neck is a five-piece laminate of maple and mahogany, which Jim Olson reckons adds a lot to the tone. The SJ shape resembles a Martin OM style, but a little deeper and curvier. The sound is warm, with masses of sustain, and will respond to picking or strumming equally well. Jim Olson is one of the finest guitar builders today and, making only about 60 guitars a year, he has quite a waiting list.

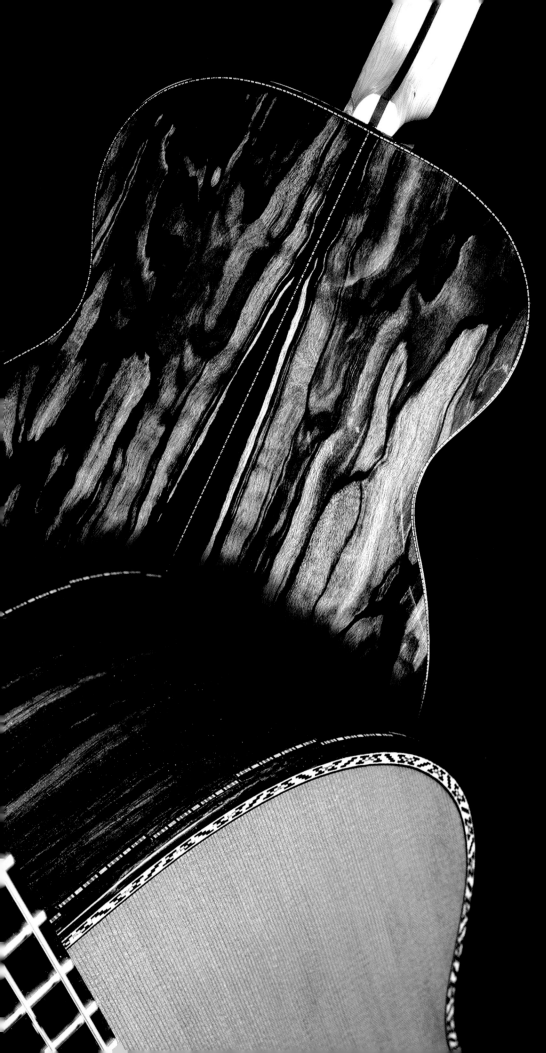

THE ACOUSTIC FLAT TOP:
MODERN BRITISH LUTHIERS

Fylde Oberon

Roger Bucknall spent his formative years in Birmingham and started making guitars in his father's garage at the age of nine. He continued making guitars as a hobby through technical school and a degree in engineering, until 1973, when he moved to the Fylde coast of Lancashire to set up his company. In 1996 the business moved to the Lake District. His list of clients includes: Pete Townshend, Keith Richards, John Renbourn and John McLaughlin. The Oberon is one of Fylde's top-line guitars, and has been used by many of Britain's leading players. Engelmann spruce is used for the top, Indian rosewood for the back and sides, ebony for the fingerboard and bridge. These guitars produce a rich sound, with lots of volume and projection. All Fylde guitars are handcrafted, resulting in a fairly small output from the workshop.

Brook Clyst

Handmade in the West Country, Brook guitars are named after local rivers. Andy and Simon produce only about 100 guitars a year, from only the finest solid woods. The Clyst is a parlour-sized guitar with a scale length of 24 7/8 in (63 cm), a 12-fret neck and slotted headstock. Built to the buyer's requirements, the '010' trim specification includes unbound headstock and fingerboard and mother-of-pearl fingerboard marker dots. The '015' specification has bound headstock and fingerboard, diamond and dot markers and gold hardware. All are built from solid woods, with wooden bindings and ebony fingerboards.

Lowden Size O-32

Lowden guitars are handmade in Northern Ireland. In specially built workshops, a hand-picked team of about 10 luthiers, trained by George Lowden himself, produces some of the most prized, high-end acoustic guitars in the world. If you have many thousands of pounds, and can wait more than two years for a guitar, George still makes a small number himself. The Original or 'O' series

guitars feature a sitka spruce top, Indian rosewood back and sides, wood and abalone rosette, and maple binding. A large, lightweight and distinctively shaped body, constructed using split woods, gives the guitar huge power, both when fingerpicking or strumming. The O-32 has the legendary Lowden string balance, with deep basses and full trebles.

THE CLASSICAL AND FLAMENCO GUITAR

Antonio de Torres

Antonio de Torres Jurado was born in La Canada de San Urbano, Almería on 13 June 1817, and is as revered among guitarists as Stradivari is among violinists. His work established the shape, design and construction of the modern guitar. Torres reasoned that the soundboard was the key to increasing the volume of the guitar, so he not only made his instruments larger than the nineteenth-century French instruments, but fitted them with thinner, lighter soundboards that were arched in both directions, made possible by a system of fan-bracing for strength. The larger body meant that the vibrating string length could be increased to 25 $^5/_8$ in (65 cm) – now the standard for classical guitars – and the fingerboard could be broader. Torres guitars are divided into two periods: the first belonging to his time in Seville from 1852 to 1870, and the second being the years from 1871 to 1893 in Almería. Usually made with spruce tops, with backs and sides of cypress, the guitars are not loud by modern standards but have a clear, balanced, firm and rounded tone. By the time of his death in 1892 at the age of 75, Torres had made over 155 guitars, although his biographer, José Romanillos, estimated that Torres might have made as many as 320 instruments during his two active periods, of which 66 have been traced.

Ignacio Fleta e Hijos

Fleta is regarded by many as the greatest guitar maker of the twentieth century. Born in Huesca, in the north-eastern Spanish region of Catalonia, on 31 July 1897, he established his own business in 1927 working on lutes, bowed instruments and guitars. In 1955 Fleta heard a radio broadcast of Segovia playing a Bach transcription, and was so impressed that he decided to dedicate the rest of his life to building guitars. Two years later he made the first of three guitars which Segovia was to perform on. Ignacio's fame grew rapidly, but as he only built 16 guitars a year his waiting list became so long that it was virtually impossible to obtain a guitar from him directly. Many of the greatest guitarists of the last few decades have been associated with his instruments, including John Williams, Alexandre Lagoya, Eduardo Falu and Alberto Ponce.

Hermann Hauser

Hermann Hauser Sr (1882–1952) was one of the great luthiers of the twentieth century, and is best remembered for the sublime instruments that he built in the Spanish tradition after 1924. In that year both Segovia and Miguel Llobet visited Hauser's workshop in Munich. Segovia encouraged Hauser to copy his 1912 Ramírez guitar (an instrument widely believed to have been made by Santos Hernández while he was foreman of the Ramírez shop), and Llobet owned an 1859 de Torres, giving Hauser the opportunity to examine that as well. Hauser began building in the Spanish style in 1925, but it was to be another 12 years before he had unlocked the secrets of the great master builders. He finally completed the instrument that Segovia had been seeking in 1936. The Maestro used the guitar extensively over the next 25 years, calling it 'the greatest guitar of our epoch', and it can be heard on many of his famous recordings. Hausers are among the most sought-after of all classical guitars.

Manuel Ramírez

Born in 1864, Manuel Ramírez de Galarreta y Planell became a far more famous guitar maker than his older brother José Ramírez I, the founder of the Ramírez dynasty. Manuel learned his skills from his brother José, and in 1882 the two of them decided to open a workshop on Cava Baja in the Rastro of Madrid. In 1890 Manuel decided to open his own workshop and said he was going to move to Paris. His brother helped him make the preparations but instead of going to Paris Manuel opened his new business in the nearby Plaza Santa Ana. Manuel and José never spoke to each other again. In 1893 Manuel won a medal at the Chicago Fair for his work, and in 1904 he had become the luthier for the Royal Conservatory of Music in Madrid (a fact that he advertised on his labels from then on). Ramírez taught many young luthiers during this period, including Santos Hernández and Domingo Esteso. Although it was his brother José who developed the 'tablao' guitar design, it was Manuel who perfected it, and it is still the model for today's Spanish classical guitar. In 1912 a young man called at the Ramírez workshop hoping to rent a guitar for a concert performance he was about to give. After hearing the young man's prodigious talent Manuel gave him the guitar as a gift. The youngster was Segovia and the guitar is now in the Metropolitan Museum of New York.

Santos Hernández

Santos Hernández Rodríguez was born in Madrid in 1873. At the age of 10 he began an apprenticeship making vestments and ornaments in a shop that sold religious paraphernalia. After a short while he left and went to work for José Ortega in Granada, but soon returned to Madrid to work in the prestigious workshop of Francisco González. In 1893 Santos was drafted into an artillery unit to serve his five years' military service, during which time he was sent to Cuba to fight in the Spanish–American war. On leaving the army in 1898 he went to work for Manuel Ramírez, and it was here that he built the guitar that is generally believed to be the one that Ramírez gave to a young Andrés Segovia in 1912. After Ramírez' death in 1916 Hernández continued working for his widow, before opening his own workshop in La Aduana, in the centre of Madrid, building both classical and flamenco guitars. Santos did not share his guitar-making secrets, and always refused to take on disciples. His instruments have been played by such distinguished classical guitarists as Luis Sánchez Granada, Regino Sainz de la Maza and Quintin Esquembre, and flamenco players Ramón Montoya, Niño Ricardo, Sabicas and Manolo Sanlúcar.

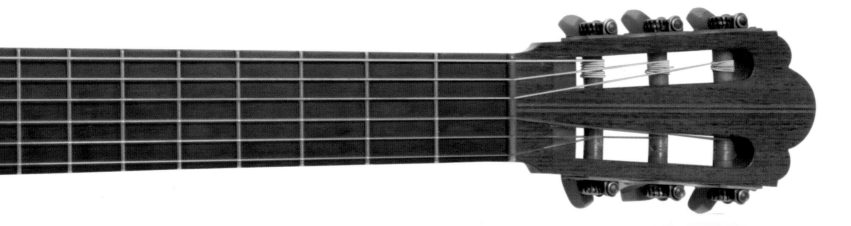

THE ACOUSTIC ARCHTOP

Gibson L-5

The L-5 was first introduced in 1922 by Gibson Guitar Corporation, then of Kalamazoo, Michigan, under the direction of master luthier Lloyd Loar, and has been in production ever since. It is now considered to be one of the most important and influential archtops ever made. Priced at $275 this top-of-the-line guitar was by far the most expensive in the company's line-up. The L-5 was Gibson's first guitar with f-holes, had a 16-in (40.6-cm) wide body (changed to 17 in/45.7 cm in 1934), with an arched spruce top and birch back (maple in 1924); a maple neck with an ebony fingerboard and a metal tailpiece. Possessing a huge, well-balanced sound, tone quality and playability, this Gibson quickly became America's first orchestral guitar, producing enough power to compete with the other instruments. The L-5 was taken up by many very influential guitar players, including Eddie Lang, Wes Montgomery, Lonnie Johnson and Maybelle Carter (whose 1928 model is now in the Country Music Hall of Fame in Nashville).

Gibson Super 400

In 1934 Gibson addressed the need for more power and volume from their guitars by introducing the top-of-the-line Super 400. As it took its name from the $400 price tag (a considerable amount of money in the Depression years), it's not surprising that very few of these ultra-deluxe guitars left the factory – so few in their debut year that no factory records exist. In 1936 only 63 Super 400s were built and in the following year only 29. (In his book on the model, Thomas VanHoose estimates a total of only 92 first-version guitars, suggesting a zero output for 1934). It had an 18-in (45.7-cm) wide, X-braced top, maple back and sides, seven-ply top binding, an ebony fingerboard with single and double split-block inlays, five-piece split diamond peghead inlay, Grover gold-plated tuners, and was finished in Cremona brown sunburst. It was eagerly embraced by professional guitarists employed by radio stations, movie studios and by big bands playing pre-war jazz and popular music. Super 400s were discontinued in 1983, then re-introduced in 1994.

Epiphone Emperor

The Emperor became Epiphone's top-of-the-line archtop guitar when introduced in late 1936, to compete with the popular Gibson Super 400. It was apparently so named because Epiphone wanted a 'royal' word to tie in with the news of Edward VIII's abdication. These superb instruments featured an 18 ½-in (47-cm) wide spruce top with three-ply binding on the f-holes, maple back and sides, ebony fingerboard, gold-plated parts and a sunburst finish. These guitars are now widely sought-after.

Epiphone Deluxe

This superb guitar was Epiphone's top-line flat-top instrument in 1931. Made to compete with the Gibson L-5, it was slightly larger at 16 3/8 in (41.7 cm), had a spruce top, maple back and sides, rosewood single-bound fingerboard, bound peghead and gold-plated parts. The high-quality finish was complemented with the Masterbilt headstocks decorated with the pretty 'wandering vine' design, and fingerboards with the distinctive floral, cloud and diamond-shaped inlays. Sales of this very expensive guitar were initially slow due to the Depression. As a result of its slightly smaller size, many guitarists found the Deluxe an easier instrument to play than the mighty Emperor of 1936 that became the premier guitar of the Epiphone range.

Stromberg Master 400

Company founder Charles Stromberg had emigrated from Sweden to Boston, Massachusetts, and after working as an instrument maker in a local workshop he formed his own business around 1905. His son Elmer joined the firm as an apprentice five years later. Elmer's early reputation was soon made as a banjo designer, before he moved to archtop guitar building in the early 1930s, as the popularity of the banjo declined. Stromberg Sr continued making drums and banjos. The Stromberg Master 400, measuring a gigantic 19 in (48.3 cm), is considered by many to be the ultimate orchestral guitar. It is the 'Holy Grail' to guitar collectors. Remarkably, the early 400s had pressed arched tops and laminated backs and sides, at a time when Gibson, Epiphone and D'Angelico were using solid carved wood. Around 1940 design changes included carved and graduated tops, three-piece f-holes replaced one-piece and – one of the most important innovations – the use of a single diagonal bar running across the inside of the instrument's soundboard. These instruments were the choice of Freddie Green with the Count Basie Orchestra, Frank Bittles of the Fletcher Henderson Orchestra and Fred Guy from Duke Ellington's band, among others, who needed massive power and projection to cut through a brass band or full orchestra without the need for amplification. The power and projection of these guitars is unsurpassed by any other archtop acoustic.

D'Angelico New Yorker

Archtop guitars by John D'Angelico are among the finest, highly rated and sought-after instruments of their kind. D'Angelico opened his workshop in Kenmare Street, New York, in 1932 and began building guitars based on the Gibson L-5. By 1937 he was able to offer his customers a choice of four guitar models – Style A, Style B, the Excel and the New Yorker. All D'Angelico instruments were strictly handmade and in limited quantities. In the late 1930s, with production at its peak, he was only able to make 35 guitars a year, with the aid of two assistants – the first being Jimmy DiSerio, who left in 1959. In the last five years of his life his only regular employee was Jimmy D'Aquisto, who began work with him in 1951 and played an increasingly important role in the company as D'Angelico's health deteriorated. It is with the Excel and New Yorker that D'Angelico's considerable reputation rests. The New Yorker, being the largest, most elaborate and costly, closely resembled the Gibson Super 400, even using similar split-box fingerboard inlays. It had an 18-in (45.7-cm) wide body, X-braced spruce top, curly maple back and sides, maple neck and ebony fretboard, triple bound f-holes, black binding lines on the body sides and the side of the fingerboard, gold-plated parts, and the peghead was decorated with the lovely, art-deco skyscraper logo and urn-shaped finial. The close relationship between D'Angelico and his customers meant that he was able to make variations as directed by individual players. D'Angelico instruments are not noted for their exceptional volume or power but produce a fantastically smooth, mellow tone, excellent sustain, and such balance that each note on the fretboard is almost equal in volume. Only 1164 D'Angelico guitars were made before John's death in 1964 and his guitars now sell for a premium, with models on display in the art-deco departments of many museums throughout the World.

D'Angelico Excel

The Excel was D'Angelico's equivalent to the Gibson L-5. Available in late
1934 the first Excels had a 17-in (43.2-cm) X-braced body – slightly larger
than the New Yorker – carved spruce top, maple back and sides, curved
single-bound f-holes, multiple-bound top and back, and block pearl
fingerboard inlays similar to the L-5. Like the New Yorker, these
guitars have become extremely collectable.

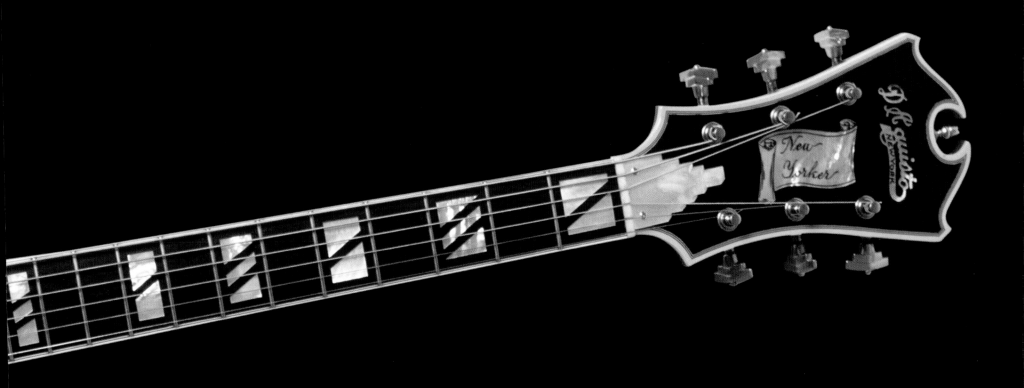

D'Aquisto New Yorker

Jimmy D'Aquisto was born on 9 November 1935, and served his apprenticeship with John D'Angelico. Following the latter's death in 1964, D'Aquisto branched out on his own and continued making his mentor's classic archtop designs, the New Yorker and Excel, under his own name. Around 1967, Jimmy developed a number of innovations, including adjustable tailpieces, smaller pickguards, and re-designed pickguards. His elegant and sleek designs, as well as the dynamic range and rich tonal quality of his guitars made them treasured favourites of serious guitarists and collectors. D'Aquisto also believed that ornamentation, such as pearl and abalone inlays, detracted from the guitar's tone. Jimmy was considered to be the finest luthier in the world, with his archtops selling, before his untimely death in 1995, for $40,000. His guitars are now among the most highly prized instruments, currently fetching well over six figures.

RESONATORS

National Tricone

The need to boost the acoustic guitar's sound had been addressed in various ways by modern makers. One of the most interesting was a guitar fitted with three resonators, invented by John Dopyera in 1927. Vaudeville performer George Beauchamp approached Dopyera with a view to making a guitar that could be heard from the stage. What Dopyera eventually came up with was the 'tri-cone' guitar, with a metal body and an aluminium, T-shaped bridge, topped with wood and mounted over a set of three aluminium resonators. As soon as Dopyera had filed the patent for the guitar, it went into production, and in 1928 Beauchamp and the Dopyera brothers founded the National String Instrument Corporation. The Tricone instruments have three 6-in (15.2-cm) cones set into a triangle, two on the bass side, and one on the treble. A T-shaped bridge connects these cones. A maple saddle sits on top of the T-bridge. The vibration from the strings travels through the saddle, which vibrates the bridge and then the three cones. This produces a very sweet and warm tone, with more harmonics than a single resonator guitar.

National Single Cone

In 1928 National introduced a guitar using just one resonator. This was another of John Dopyera's ideas but George Beauchamp claimed it was his and filed a patent under his own name. The following hostilities split the company apart, with the Dopyeras eventually winning the lawsuit that ousted Beauchamp from the National board. The National Single Cone has a convex 9 1/2-in (24.1-cm) diameter maple 'biscuit' on top of the cone. The biscuit has a maple saddle, which the strings pass over but unlike an ordinary acoustic flat top, where the vibration of the wooden body creates the sound, the string vibration goes through the saddle and the bridge to the cone, causing it to resonate and amplify the sound. Single cone guitars are louder than tricones and have a sharp attack with a short sustain, not unlike a banjo.

Dobro

In 1929, following the hostilities between the Dopyera brothers and George Beauchamp over the National Single Cone guitar patents, John Dopyera took his original design, turned the resonator upside down and modified its V shape into a W. A rotating spider connected to the bridge carried the sound to the edges of the cone. The inverted resonator enabled the guitar to sustain notes for longer than on the biscuit-bridge cone. Rudy and Ed Dopyera left National and joined John to set up a new company called Dobro – a shortened version of DOpyera BROthers (the word also means 'good' in their native Slovak language). Most Dobros have wooden bodies but Dobro also made metal-bodied guitars from 1935 to 1940 only.

National Reso-Phonic

National Reso-Phonic Guitars was set up in the late 1980s by Don Young and McGregor Gaines, dedicated to reproducing the look, sound and feel of the old National guitars. In addition to their faithful reproductions of great vintage instruments, National Reso-Phonic are creating new looks, louder sounds and better serviceability than ever before.

National Reso-Phonic Style O

This is a single resonator guitar with a nickel-plated brass body featuring an etched Hawaiian design and rolled f-holes, maple neck, a bound ebony fretboard with 12 frets to the body and a slotted headstock (*see* next page). It has a warm, bluesy tone and the looks of the old National guitars.

THE SEMI-ACOUSTIC GUITAR

In the 1930s guitarists, particularly those having to compete with the horns and drums of an orchestra, needed more volume from their instruments. A number of makers began to market semi-acoustic guitars, Gibson being the first, with its 'Electric Spanish' ES-150. These were basically conventionally shaped archtops but with an electric pickup and controls built into the body. Semi-acoustics are extremely versatile, and have been used in a wide range of musical styles, for example Chuck Berry's rock 'n' roll style on a Gibson ES-335, B. B. King's blues on a 335, Chet Atkins' country with a Gretsch Country Gentleman, Noel Gallagher on an Epiphone Sheraton, and, of course, John Lennon's use of the Epiphone Casino.

Gibson ES-150

The ES-150 (ES – Electric Spanish) is generally recognized as the world's first commercially feasible electric guitar. It was designated 150 because it cost $150. After its introduction in 1936, it immediately became popular in the jazz orchestras of the period. Guitarist Eddie Durham is usually credited with making the first electric guitar solo in 1936 on an ES-150, but the most important player of the instrument is Charlie Christian. He was quick to exploit the ES-150's capabilities. With wonderful breaks and warm, flowing solos, he revolutionized jazz guitar playing. The L-150's pickup, later called the Charlie Christian, had one solid, straight pole piece and two magnets. The body was a 16-in (40.6-cm) solid spruce archtop with mahogany back and sides, mahogany neck with rosewood fingerboard, and a 24-in (61-cm) scale.

In the late 1940s, after some experiments earlier in the decade, Gibson started production of the electric guitar. The ES-175 debuted in 1949. With a comfortable body and a stylish pointed cutaway, it quickly became the most popular guitar of the jazz world, used by such players as Pat Metheny and Joe Pass. It had a 16-in (40.6-cm) body with a maple/poplar/maple laminate top, which gave the 175 its distinctive sound. The neck was mahogany with a rosewood fingerboard and pearl split inlays. The first incarnation had one single-coil P90 pickup in the neck position. In 1953 the ES175D, a two-pickup model, was introduced. These humbuckers gave the guitar a full, rich tone.

Gibson ES-350

Launched in 1947, this was the first of the new-style Gibson electrics. It was also the first electric Gibson with a cutaway. The early versions had a single pickup, later replaced with two pickups. With the introduction of the ES-350, Gibson crafted an entire guitar from pressed maple laminates.

Gibson ES-5

Introduced in 1949, the triple pickup ES-5 was the most elaborate guitar that Gibson had ever produced. In 1955 the guitar was re-named the Switchmaster and had separate volume and tone controls for each pickup, as well as a four-way selector switch that allowed each pickup to be selected either individually or in trio configuration. Later models were fitted with humbucker pickups.

Gibson L-5CES

In 1951 Gibson launched full electric versions of their ES-175 and Super 400 guitars. These were the L-5CES (CES – Cutaway Electric Spanish) and Super 400CES respectively. The L-5CES featured a single rounded cutaway, 17-in (43.2-cm) wide-bound hollow body, solid carved spruce top, layered tortoise pickguard, maple back, sides and neck, a 20-fret bound ebony fingerboard with pearl block inlay, model name-engraved trapeze tailpiece, and the peghead with pearl flame inlay. The electrics consisted of two P90 single coil pickups (alnico in 1954, humbucker in 1957), two volume and two tone controls, and a three-position switch. The L-5CES was a great favourite with Elvis's guitarist Scotty Moore, who traded up from the ES-295 in 1955, 'mainly because the workmanship was so much better in the L-5. Of course it cost more too' ($565). Best known of the jazz guitarists to play the L-5 was Wes Montgomery, who drew a mellow sound from it, thanks to his distinctive

Gibson Super 400CES

Launched along with the L-5CES in 1951, the Super 400 had an 18-in (45.7-cm) wide and 4-in (10.2-cm) deep body. It was the bulk of the body that made it slightly less popular with guitarists than the L-5. It had a top of bookmatched solid spruce, maple back, sides and neck, solid ebony fingerboard with mother-of-pearl block inlay, seven-ply body binding and triple-bound f-holes. The original hardware included two P-90 pickups, changed to humbuckers in 1957. The Super 400CES was top of the Gibson electric guitar line, and unlike previous Gibson electrics, the CES guitars were made of carved solid spruce, giving a richer and more complex tone than the laminated models of earlier years. Players of this guitar have included Kenny Burrell, Merle Travis, Larry Coryell and Pee Wee Crayton.

Gibson Byrdland

The Byrdland, one of the most distinctive acoustic-electric guitars in Gibson history, was originally designed in collaboration with country-jazz guitarists Bill Byrd and Hank Garland in 1955. While it featured the same spruce top and maple sides as the L-5, the Byrdland's overall depth of two in (5.1 cm) is thinner than the more traditional 3 ³/₈ in (8.6 cm) of the L-5. This new thinline guitar also featured a short scale neck of only 23 in (58.4 cm), which eased playing and facilitated more intricate single-note patterns, and allowed guitarists to use unusual stretched chords. The Byrdland had a solid spruce top, maple back and sides, ebony fingerboard and gold hardware. The single-coil pickup was replaced with humbuckers in 1957.

Gibson ES-335

The ES-335 was the first commercial semi-hollowbody electric guitar released by Gibson in 1958. It is neither hollow nor solid; instead it has a solid block of wood running through the centre of its otherwise hollow body. This design enabled guitarists to address the problem of the terrible feedback that occurred when ordinary hollow-body guitars were played at high volume, caused by the pickups picking up their own sound and feeding it back to the system. The distinctive 'woody' sound, mellower than solid-bodies, high sustain and low feedback have made these guitars popular in nearly all genres of modern music. The 335 had a maple laminated body, with double symmetrical cutaways, incorporating a solid maple centre block, mahogany neck and rosewood fretboard. With a basic price of $267.50, it rapidly became a bestseller, and has been in continuous production since its launch.

Gibson ES-355

At about the same time that the ES-335 was launched, Gibson introduced the similar ES-355, featuring the symmetrical cutaway shape, a solid block of wood running through the centre of the body to cut down feedback, and the new thinline dimensions. Also on offer was stereo wiring and a six-way selector switch called the 'Varitone'. This was a tone-altering circuit developed by Gibson's pickup expert, Walt Fuller, but it proved unpopular with players, and many guitars had the Varitone wiring removed. The most famous of the ES-355s is the great blues guitarist B. B. King's 'Lucille'. The guitar has a body of maple/poplar/maple, with a solid one-piece maple block running through the centre of the guitar, and this is where the punch, bite and sustain of the instrument comes from. The guitar has a rich bass, pronounced mid-range and stinging bite.

Epiphone Sheraton

In 1957 Gibson purchased the Epiphone Company, who up until that time had been one of Gibson's fiercest rivals – particularly in the field of hollowbody archtops. Under orders from Ted McCarthy to produce some new Epiphone models for the upcoming NAMM show (an annual music trade fair in California) in 1958, Gibson introduced a new line, highlighted by the Sheraton. With its semi-hollowbody construction, similar to that of the Gibson ES-335, the Sheraton had a more stylish look, emphasized by its Emperor-style V-block fingerboard inlays, and vine inlay on the peghead. The thinline body was made of maple, with a mahogany neck and rosewood fingerboard. The Sheraton was an immediate hit; the unique voice of its mini humbuckers soon made it the instrument of choice for many leading guitarists of the time, including blues legend John Lee Hooker.

Epiphone Casino

The Epiphone Casino is a thinline hollowbody guitar based on the Gibson ES-330, and is traditionally regarded as a budget version of this guitar. However, the guitar's association with guitarists such as John Lennon and Noel Gallagher has caused the popularity of the Casino to rise, and it is now considered a classic in its own right. Equipped with two Gibson P90 pickups, it is known for its heavy sound, which makes it an ideal rhythm guitar. The sound is generally thinner and more trebly than the 335, and due to its hollow body, more prone to feedback. Paul McCartney used a Casino for some of his studio recording sessions, including guitar solos on 'Drive my Car' and 'Taxman'. John Lennon and George Harrison also bought Casinos around 1965. John used his as his main instrument, in preference to his Rickenbacker 325, during the remainder of his time with the Beatles. He can be seen using it at the Apple rooftop concert, and in the film *Let It Be*. Other notable players of the Epiphone Casino have been Paul Weller, Tom Petty and The Edge.

Gretsch White Falcon

In early 1954 Gretsch marketing strategist Jimmie Webster wanted to design a guitar to be better than the top-of-the-line Gibson Super 400. A one-off guitar, the White Falcon, was unveiled at the NAMM show of 1954, and displayed as 'The Guitar of the Future', with Gretsch having no plans to manufacture the model. With its immense 17-in (43.2-cm) wide by 2 3/4-in (6.9-cm) deep white body, highest quality gold-plated hardware, engraved pearl inlays, and sparkly gold bindings, the guitar was nicknamed 'The Cadillac of Guitars'. Such was the interest in this fabulous guitar that Gretsch decided to manufacture it as their top model in 1955, with the advertising slogan, 'The finest guitar we know how to make – and what a beauty!' Cost at the time – a whopping $600. The original model had two DynaSonic single coil pickups; controls consisting of master tone, master volume, volume for each pickup, and a three-way toggle pickup selector. The single cutaway body was solid spruce, laminated back and sides with gold sparkle, white/black/white binding, ebony fretboard and a falcon in mid-flight engraved on the pickguard. Various changes have been made: a stereo version in 1959; double cutaway in 1963; and in 1965 a number of knobs and switches were added affording access to new tonal variations. Notable White Falcon players have included Steven Stills, Neil Young and John Frusciante.

Gretsch 6119 Tennessean

The Tennessean debuted in 1958 as, essentially, a one-pickup, stripped-down 6120. While it lacked much of the ornamentation of the 6120, the single cutaway body did have real f-holes, a Bigsby B-6 tailpiece, one FilterTron in the bridge position, an orange finish, and black pickguard. The switchgear consisted of a one-volume knob and one-tone switch. 1962 saw the introduction of a much thinner 1 $7/8$-in (4.6-cm) body, painted-on f-holes, a darker cherry red or mahogany finish and rosewood replacing ebony on the neck. New circuitry and twin HiLoTron pickups replaced the single pickup. The pickguard was changed to the more familiar silver type.

Gretsch 6120 Chet Atkins Hollow Body

The Gretsch 6120, a hollowbody guitar with f-holes, first appeared in the mid 1950s with the endorsement of Chet Atkins. Eddie Cochran, Duane Eddy and many others quickly adopted it. When introduced, the 6120 cost $385 and was highly decorated, with a cow's head and cactus etchings in the block markers, and a large 'G' brand on the amber red top. In 1958 the half-moon fret markers common to most Gretsch guitars were introduced, and the DeArmond pickups were changed to Gretsch's own 'FilterTron' humbuckers. Chet Atkins said that Duane Eddy was the only guitarist that ever got a good tone out of the DeArmonds. The introduction specification included: 16-in (40.6-cm) wide, 2 $7/8$-in (7.1-cm) thick maple body, bound f-holes, double-bound top and back, single-bound rosewood fingerboard and peghead. There were one tone and two volume knobs on the lower bout, one master volume knob on the cutaway and one pickup selector on the upper bout.

Gretsch 6122 Country Gentleman

Considered by many to be one of the 'holy trinity' of Gretsch guitars, along with the 6120 and White Falcon, The Gentleman appeared in 1957 – after considerable input from Chet Atkins – and was priced between the 6120 and Falcon in price. It had a 17-in (43.2-cm) by 2-in (5.1 cm) thick single cutaway body, with fake cutaway f-holes on the mahogany finished top. Atkins wanted Gretsch to produce a semi-hollow guitar with a solid block through the middle, like Gibson's ES-335, to reduce feedback. This didn't happen, although the 6122s did get a partial block. In 1962 the Gentleman adopted Gretsch's 'Electrotone' double cutaway body, and it was one of these that George Harrison made famous. George can be heard playing it on a number of sessions, including; 'With The Beatles', 'A Hard Day's Night', 'Beatles For Sale', and 'Help'.

Gretsch 6118 Double Anniversary

Introduced in 1958 as a celebration of Gretsch's founding. Although 'promotionally priced', the original Anniversarys are considered to be the ultimate model of the series. As the 1960s commenced, Gretsch began moving the guitar gradually downscale: rosewood replaced ebony on the fingerboards and HiLoTron single coils replaced FilterTrons. One of the colours offered to purchasers was the beautiful two-tone smoke green: a light green top and

Rickenbacker 330

A six-string hollowbody with a scimitar-shaped sound hole, double cutaway, two pickups and dot inlays. The 330SF had unusual features, even for a Rickenbacker. The nuts, frets, pickups and bridge were all slanted, to match precisely the natural angle of the fretting fingers. This experimental guitar was a commercial flop and the company reverted to a conventional layout.

Rickenbacker 325

The distinctive sweeping shape of Rickenbacker's most famous hollowbody electric guitars was quite unlike anything being produced by any of their competitors. The 300 is a series of semi-acoustic guitars launched in 1958, shortly after F. C. Hall took over the company. The 325 features a 20-in. (50.8-cm) short scale, dot fretboard inlays and a small, 12-in (30.5-cm) wide body. The body is unbound, semi-hollow maple (without a soundhole), and boasts crescent-moon type cutaways. The instruments were equipped with two volume switches, two tone switches, one blend switch, and a toggle to switch between pickups. Necks were maple. The 325 gained prominence due to John Lennon's use of the guitar during the early years of the Beatles. Lennon owned at least four 325s, the first of which, a natural-blond model with a Kauffman vibrato, he bought in Hamburg. He had the guitar refinished in black, and used it on all recordings and in all concerts until early 1964. (Listen to John playing rhythm on 'All My Loving'.) Rickenbacker provided Lennon with an updated black version in 1964.

Rickenbacker 331

These bizarre 'light show' guitars were made in the early 1970s. Based on the 330 model, they had a body made of clear plastic with coloured lights inside. These lit up as the guitar reached particular frequencies. Early models were hand-wired, with two rows of bulbs arranged in straight lines. Later models used a printed circuit board with much brighter bulbs spaced out across the interior.

Rickenbacker 360

The 360 model was a deluxe version of the 330, with stereo output, a bound fretboard and soundhole and triangle inlays. Earlier models have a 330 body shape, with top and bottom binding and no soundhole binding.

Rickenbacker 360-12

Overshadowed by Gibson's and Fender's, Rickenbacker electric guitars were obscure until the early 1960s, when John Lennon began using the 325 model. Soon after, George Harrison obtained an early 12-string version, as did Roger McGuinn of the Byrds, who used it to create his trademark jingle-jangle sound. First made in 1964, the 360-12 was one of the earliest electric twelve-string guitars. It was constructed of a slim, semi-hollow maple body and a set-in maple neck, with a rosewood fretboard inlaid with white triangles. The hardware consisted of two volume, two tone and one balance switches, a three-way selector and two single-coil pickups. The Rickenbacker uses an unconventional headstock design that incorporates both a slotted-style peghead, and a solid peghead, thereby eliminating the need for the large headstock normally found on a twelve-string guitar. Another unique feature of the 360-12 was the ordering of the courses. Most twelve-strings have the octave course on the bass side of the standard course; the Rickenbacker reverses this convention, resulting in a big chorusing sound, like that of two guitars playing together at once. Other notable players have included Tom Petty, Chris Martin of Coldplay, and Marty Willson-Piper of The Church.

Rickenbacker 365

The 365 was part of the Rickenbacker deluxe line-up. It was essentially a
Rickenbacker 360 with a vibrato option. It was available in 'OS' or 'NS' styles.

THE ELECTRO ACOUSTIC GUITAR

Ovation Balladeer

For bands on tour in the 1960s, amplification of their acoustic guitars on stage was a huge problem. A microphone in front of the guitar bound the performer to one spot. An electric pickup in an acoustic guitar ruined the sound quality of the instrument. None of these worked if there were electric instruments or drums in the band. In 1966, Charles Kaman, an engineer who had founded an aircraft company, introduced his first round-back guitar. Having been advised that a guitar made of a synthetic material would be unmarketable, he experimented with high-tech sonic equipment, and invented the one-piece Lyrachord body shell, made from fibres that were used to cover helicopter blades. Ovation then built a special type of six-way pickup into the bridge, which reacted to the vibration of both the strings and the spruce top. Played through an amplifier, the sound was very like that of an acoustic guitar. One of the most popular and visible guitarists in the late 1960s was Glen Campbell. Every week Glen and his Ovation could be seen by millions of Americans as they tuned into 'The Glen Campbell Goodtime Hour'.

Ovation Adamas

Introduced in 1976, the Adamas (Latin for diamond) was Ovation's
top-of-the-line guitar. Furthering the use of synthetic materials, the
top was made from a sandwich of $1/32$-in (8-mm)-thick birch and
thinner layers of carbon graphite fibres. Ovation had discovered
that a carbon fibre/graphite combination had all the right
characteristics: it was lightweight and strong, and yet
resonant like spruce and, better still, it was impervious
to changes in temperature and humidity. A series of
22 small soundholes at the body's top end gave the
guitar a bright tone and better projection than the
traditional central round hole. Surrounding the
soundholes was a leaf-shaped epaulette of exotic
woods. Such players as Glen Campbell, Al Di
Meola, and Rick Nielsen used the Adamas.

Takamine TNV460SC

Takamine has been building guitars at its factory, nestled at the base of Takamine Mountain, for over 40 years, and has developed into one of the world's leading guitar manufacturers. In 1978 the company began to introduce acoustic-electric guitars into the marketplace. One of Takamine's great advancements was the development of their palathetic pickup, a system of six individual piezo transducers embedded in the bridge plate, where they pick up the vibration from both string and soundboard. The TNV460SC is one of Takamine's top-of-the-line models. The cutaway tops are solid 'bear-claw' spruce, while the back and sides are solid bookmatched Indian rosewood with an ebony fingerboard. The soundhole and guitar tops are edged with abalone. This instrument is equipped with a CTP-1 Cool Tube preamp. Designed to run at very low voltages, just two or three degrees above ambient, it eliminates the danger of damage to delicate guitar woods.

Taylor 914ce

In 1974, Californian guitar luthier Bob Taylor set up a guitar-making business with a colleague, Kurt Listug, in Lemon Grove, San Diego, California. Their approach to guitar building was to combine traditional craftsmanship with high technology. With their factory in El Cajon, California, producing around 100 instruments a day, Taylor Guitars are now a major force in the industry. Although Taylor do not pay performers to endorse their instruments, or give away guitars to high-profile players, the list of artists using them is huge. The Taylor 914ce is a guitar of the very highest quality with a Grand Auditorium body and a soft, round Venetian cutaway. The top is sitka spruce, with back and sides in Indian rosewood, giving the guitar a clear tone and excellent balance, sustain and bass response. It has a mahogany neck and an ebony fretboard and headstock. The 914ce uses Taylor's own 'Expression System' pickup technology.

THE ELECTRIC GUITAR

The development of the solid-body electric guitar owes a great deal to Adolph Rickenbacker, who originally made metal components for National Resonator Guitars. He teamed up with George Beauchamp and Paul Barth who had been working together on the principle of the electric pickup. Together they founded The Electro String Instruments Corporation in 1931 and produced their first Hawaiian guitars. Their success prompted Gibson to start making electric guitars, introducing the ES150 in 1936, the first commercially acceptable instrument. During the 1940s the electric models from makers like Gibson, Epiphone and Gretsch became firmly established, but manufacturers began looking at ways of applying the solid body of Hawaiian and steel string guitars to regular instruments. In 1944 Leo Fender designed a new, small pickup that he wanted to incorporate into a solid body guitar, with a regular fretted fingerboard. 1946 saw the formation of the Fender Electric Instrument Company and the introduction of the Broadcaster, later renamed the Telecaster. At the same time Les Paul was working in the same direction. In 1941, he produced his historic 'Log' guitar. By 1954 Fender had started producing the Stratocaster, and along with the Telecaster, and the guitars that Les Paul was designing for Gibson, the standard was set for solid-body electric guitars.

Rickenbacker 'Frying Pan'

In the 1930s, American bands got their rhythm from the drums, bass and the strumming of an acoustic guitar. The problem was that no one could hear the guitar in the background over the rest of the orchestra. The Rickenbacker A22 lap steel 'Frying Pan' was the first commercially available electric guitar. Although it is called a Rickenbacker it was actually the brainchild of George Beauchamp, a talented inventor who enjoyed experimenting with the electrification of instruments. He teamed up with Adolph Rickenbacker, who was producing metal bodies for Beauchamp's National guitar company. In late 1931, Beauchamp, Rickenbacker and partners formed the Ro-Pat-In Corporation for the purpose of developing the electric guitar. The main result was an instrument with a long wooden neck and a round wooden body, housing two large 'horseshoe' magnets surrounding the strings. The principle of the electro-magnetic pickup is fairly straightforward. The vibrations from a plucked metal string will disturb a magnetic field, a current will be induced in a

coil, the coil generates an electrical signal, which is fed out of the guitar to an amplifier and speaker. The original 'Frying Pan' wooden body was changed to cast aluminium by the time production began in 1932 and came in two sizes: the A22 and the longer scale A25. Early sales of the 'Frying Pan' were poor, not least because the aluminium used caused problems with the guitar's tuning. Also the timing could not have been worse. 1931 heralded the lowest depths of the Great Depression, and few people had money to spend on guitars. In 1933 the 'Frying Pan' with amp cost an astronomical $175. By contrast a Martin D-28 Herringbone cost $100 and the Martin D-45 only $200. Although the guitar was already in production, two successive patent examiners questioned whether the instrument was 'operative'. After many delays patent was granted in 1935, by which time other manufacturers had invented and marketed guitars of their own.

MERLE TRAVIS

Gibson Les Paul Log

Born Lester Polfus in Waukesha, Milwaukee, in 1916, Les Paul's inventions would have a lasting effect on modern electric guitars. Dissatisfied with the electric guitars on sale in the mid 1930s, Paul began experimenting with a few designs of his own. What he came up with was the 'Log', which was nothing more than a piece of 4 x 4 wood, with a bridge, guitar neck and pickup attached. To this he screwed the spruce top of an Epiphone jazz guitar sawn lengthwise with the 4 x 4 block in the middle. The back was made from plywood and the bridge from a piece of steel dowel. These arrangements overcame two big problems: feedback, as the guitar no longer resonated with the amplified sound, and sustain, as the energy of the strings was not dissipated in generating sound through the guitar body. Gibson were not impressed – they called Les Paul 'the kid with the broomstick with the pickups on'. The Log now sits in the Country Music Hall of Fame in Nashville.

Bigsby/Travis

'I can build anything.' With that statement Paul Bigsby switched from building Crocker motorcycles to making musical instruments. In the 1940s Bigsby's interest in motorcycles and country music brought him into contact with Merle Travis, a country singer and guitarist, who developed the damped-picking style that influenced Chet Atkins. Travis asked Bigsby to fix the worn-out Kaufman vibrato on his Gibson L10. Paul ended up designing a whole new mechanism, which became the standard vibrato of choice for most guitar manufacturers. In 1946 Travis showed Bigsby a sketch of a solid body electric guitar, and asked if Paul could make it for him. The answer: 'I can make anything.' The guitar had all six tuning pegs on one side of the headstock (because, as Travis said, 'reaching down to change the first, second and third strings bugged me'), and a body and through-neck of birdseye maple. The back consisted of a large plastic plate, with six ferrules for anchoring the strings, which fed through from the body. This compact guitar changed the sound and look of guitars forever. It was produced in small numbers, and very few remain, making them immensely collectable. The Bigsby/Travis guitar can be seen alongside the Les Paul 'Log' in the Country Music Hall of Fame.

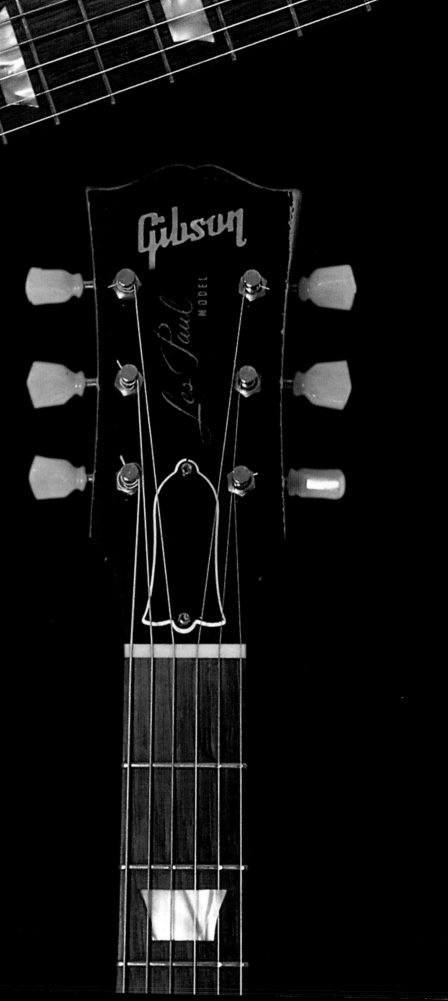

Gibson Les Paul Goldtop

The Gibson Les Paul is one of the most recognized solid-body electric guitar designs. The first version, the 'Goldtop', was introduced in 1952, with two P90 single-coil pickups and a one-piece 'trapeze'-style bridge and tailpiece. The carved body and classic Gibson headstock were borrowed from their established archtop guitars. The weight and tonal characteristics of the Les Paul were largely due to the mahogany and maple construction. The first guitars were far from perfect instruments with problems concerning intonation, neck angle and pitch. Redesign of subsequent models saw the trapeze tailpiece evolve into a 'wrap-around', and then into the current Tune-o-matic bridge. These early Goldtops are of great interest to collectors, and can sell for more money than the more practical and useable modern instruments.

Gibson Les Paul Standard

In 1958 Gibson replaced the Goldtop with the Standard model. This guitar had the more conservative sunburst finish already being used on Gibson's archtop models. Gibson continued making the Standard until 1961, when it launched the SG style instead. Only about 2,000 Standards were made between 1958 and 1961, making these guitars very sought-after. Gibson re-launched the Les Paul when guitarists discovered that, played at a high volume, it produced a thick, sustaining sound. In the hands of players like Eric Clapton and Mike Bloomfield, the model became extremely popular. The Standard appeared again in 1975 and has been in production ever since.

Gibson Les Paul Custom

The second edition of the Les Paul guitar was introduced in 1954. Called the Gibson Les Paul Custom, this entirely black guitar was an expertly decorated work of art, dubbed 'Black Beauty'. It featured a mahogany top, the new Tune-o-matic bridge, and an Alnico-5 magnet in the neck position. In 1957 the Custom was fitted with humbucker pickups. Production discontinued in 1963. In 2007 Gibson released a new edition to celebrate the annirversary of this classic.

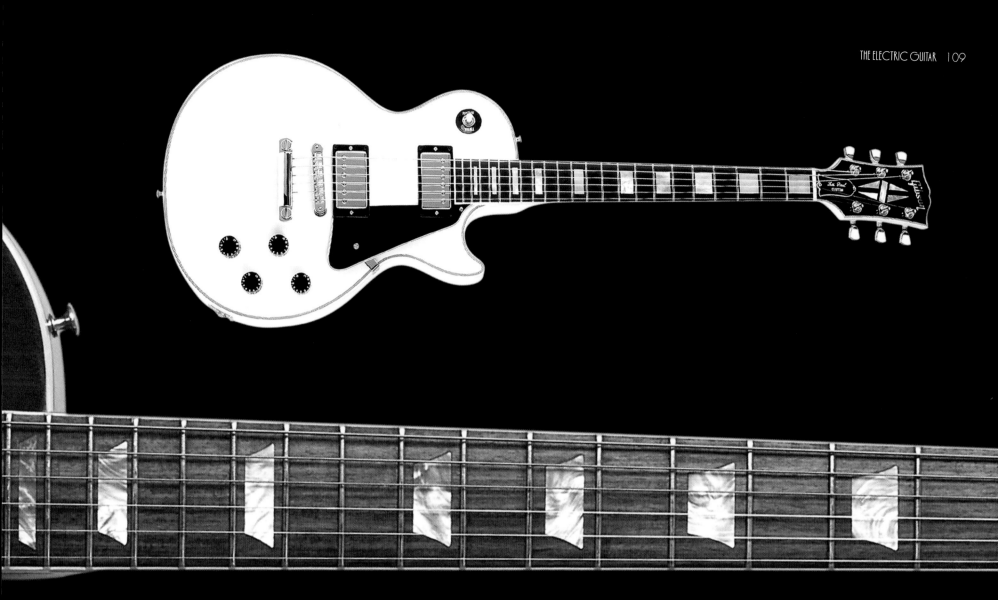

Gibson Les Paul Classic Antique

Drawing on the specifications of the earlier Les Paul guitars, Gibson are producing a 'classics' line of instruments. The Classic Antique has a figured maple top, mahogany back and neck, rosewood fingerboard and the acclaimed 1957 Classic PAF humbuckers. Players can now experience the power and performance of an original Les Paul but at an affordable price.

Gibson Les Paul Deluxe

The Deluxe was among the 'new' Les Pauls of 1968. It featured 'mini humbuckers', also known as 'New York' humbuckers, and did not initially prove popular. Interest in this particular model was so low that in the early 1980s Gibson halted production. However in 2005 the Deluxe was reintroduced with more success.

Gibson Explorer

The Explorer was first marketed in 1958, and called the Futura. It had an extreme, unconventional body design, as did Gibson's other unusual model of the time, the 'Flying V'. Its initial run was not a success, with less than 100 guitars. The scarcity of this model has increased its value enormously, and it is highly prized by collectors. Korina wood was used for the body and neck, with rosewood or ebony (on Classic White only) fretboards. Hardware included a Tune-o-matic bridge pickup, and two humbuckers. Available in Ebony, Classic White, Cherry and Natural. In 1975, Gibson began reissuing the Explorer after other companies put out similar guitars, notably Hamer, with their 'Standard', and Jackson, with their 'Kelly' line of guitars. Gibson sued Jackson Guitars over the design of the Kelly series which, apart from being sleeker and lighter, were identical to the Explorer.

Gibson SG

In 1960 Gibson experienced a decline in electric guitar sales due to their high prices and strong competition from Fender's much lighter Stratocaster. In 1961 Gibson launched a thinner and lighter Les Paul, with two sharply pointed cutaways that made the upper frets more accessible. It had a mahogany body, ebony or rosewood fretboard and one, two or three humbuckers, or one or two P90 pickups. However the design was done without Les Paul's knowledge, and he asked Gibson to remove his name from the guitar, and ended his involvement with the company. The model name was changed to SG, which stood for Solid Guitar. The SG continues to be produced to this day.

Gibson Flying V

With the rise of rock 'n' roll in the late 1950s, Gibson began to fall behind in guitar sales as players gravitated towards Fender's Stratocaster. Things changed when the company introduced its modernistic models, including the Flying V and Explorer. As a solid-body guitar produces sound through the interaction of its strings and pickups, there is no need to make it in a traditional shape to produce a decent sound. A member of staff at Gibson thought that the one fashioned after an arrow looked more like a 'flying V' ... the name stuck. The response from retailers to this radical design was completely negative, and the guitars were commercial disasters. Only 98 Flying Vs were shipped in 1958–59. In the mid-1960s guitarists such as Albert King, Lonnie Mack, Dave Davies and Jimi Hendrix started using Flying Vs, and the renewed interest created a demand for Gibson to reissue the model in 1967. The new model had a bigger, more stylish pickguard, and a stopbar tailpiece in place of the original bridge, which had strings inserted through the back.

Fender Telecaster

The Fender Telecaster was developed by Leo Fender in Fullerton, California, in the 1940s. Many other companies had tried creating a solid-body electric guitar between 1932 and 1949, but none made a significant impact on the market. Leo Fender's Telecaster finally put the solid-body guitar on the map. The Telecaster's simple and modular design was geared to mass production, and made servicing broken guitars easier. Components were produced cheaply and quickly and put together on an assembly line. Bodies were band-sawn and routed from slabs of either ash or alder, rather than hand-carved as with other guitars, such as Gibsons. The 'Tele' had a bolt-on neck that allowed it to be removed easily for servicing, repair or replacement. In addition the neck was fashioned from a single piece of maple without a separate fingerboard. The electronics were easily accessed through a removable control plate. Hardware included two single-coil pickups controlled by a three-way selector switch, and one each of volume and tone controls. The secret of the Telecaster's bright, cutting tone centres around the bridge pickup, which is wound more than the neck pickup and hence has a much higher output. A slanting-back pickup is incorporated into the bridge, enhancing the guitar's natural treble tone. Significant Telecaster players include: James Burton, Roy Buchanan, Albert Collins, Muddy Waters, Keith Richards, Bruce Springsteen and Jimmy Page.

Fender Telecaster 40th Anniversary

This special edition Telecaster was based on the American Standard model, but with several deluxe features. These included a bound tiger-striped maple body and gold hardware. Made in a limited edition of 300 copies.

Fender Telecaster Deluxe

This stylish model, available from 1972 to 1983, was a neat fusion of styling, taking elements of the Strat and forging them into a special version of the Tele. It featured a Strat bridge, Strat 70's wide headstock, strat tone switch and strat-style controls. Even with its wide humbuckers, it somehow still managed to hold that clean Telecaster twang.

Fender Telecaster Thinline

The Thinline is a Telecaster with body cavities. The semi-hollow design was
originally an attempt to reduce the weight of the solid-body electric guitar.
The f-hole and redesigned pickguard give the most apparent visual clues to
its construction. There are now two versions of the Thinline. The 1969 version
with two standard Telecaster pickups, and the 1972 version with two Fender
Wide Range pickups.

Fender Telecaster American Standard

In the 1980s Fender introduced the introduction of the revived Telecaster Standard, which bordered from other models with its lack of through-body stringing seaboard using the pressed and mounted at back. The American Standard Telecaster designed for the has this classical looks set from a classic.

Fender Stratocaster

Arguably the most copied electric guitar of all time, the Stratocaster was launched by the Fender Electric Instrument Company of Fullerton, California, in early 1954. While the Telecaster was hugely successful, many players of the day used a Bigsby vibrato device with which guitarists could bend notes up and down. Fender decided to produce a more expensively made ash or alder line of guitars with his own design of tremolo arm. Guitarists Bill Carson and Rex Gallion suggested a contoured body, rather than the harsh body of the 'Tele'. The name Stratocaster was intended to evoke images of the new jet age (such as the Boeing B-52 Stratofortress).

The Stratocaster featured three single-coil pickups, a three-way selector switch, one volume knob and two tone controls. The cost of the first guitars was $249.50. One of these early Strats was a key component of the Buddy Holly look, along with his heavy black-rimmed glasses. The neck, middle and bridge pickups provide a wide range of tones, giving the guitar great versatility. The tremolo arm mechanism has become the most copied design of all, eclipsing all others. The list of distinguished players associated with the Strat is almost endless, including Hank Marvin, Rory Gallagher, Eric Clapton, Jimi Hendrix, Mark Knopfler, George Harrison and David Gilmour.

Fender Stratocaster 1959 (Hank Marvin)

The Stratocaster was unavailable in the UK in the early 1960s but Hank Marvin, the Shadows' guitarist, played what is thought to be the first Strat in the country. Serial number 34,346 was finished in a coral pink shade of Fiesta Red, sometimes referred to as salmon pink. This guitar, with its tremolo arm, contributed to the Shadows' distinctive sound. So distinctive was this sound that many musicians – including the Beatles – initially avoided the instrument and chose other marques.

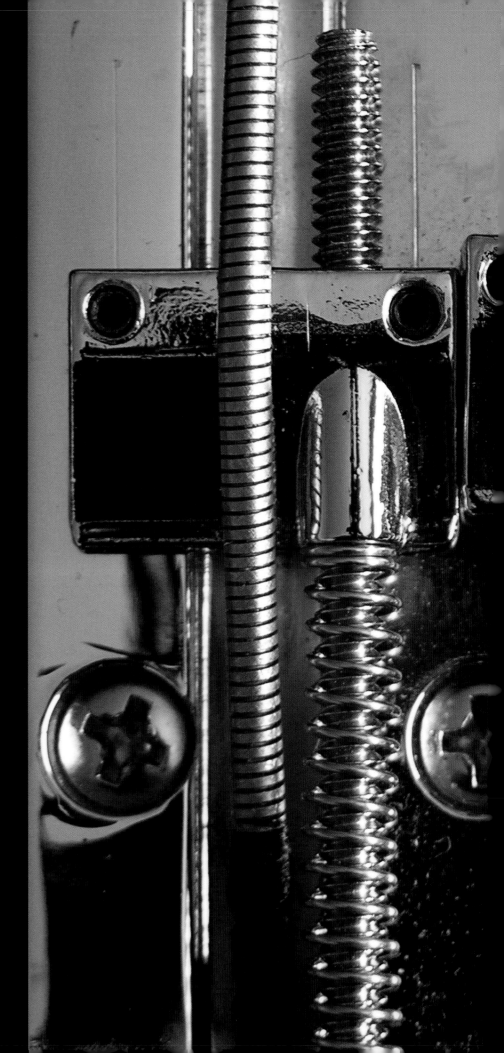

Fender Stratocaster Wide Headstock

The wide headstock was used from 1965 to 1971, when under the
ownership of CBS. For this reason alone it proved unpopular with some,
although others enjoyed the more dramatic curves of the sculpted head.

Fender Stratocaster 25th Anniversary

In 1979 Fender celebrated the 25th anniversary of the Stratocaster. The first 500 instruments were finished in pearl white. However, due to the instability of the finish and the cracking that resulted, many were recalled and finished in 'Porsche Silver' (or '25th Anniversary Stratocaster Silver', as Fender called it). The 1979 Strat featured a reversion to the four-bolt neck plate, the abandonment of the 'bullet' truss rod adjustment, and the first use of locking tuners on a Fender.

Fender Stratocaster 35th Anniversary

In 1989, Fender produced a limited edition of 500 top-quality Stratocasters to celebrate the model's 35th anniversary. Made with maple tops, they had dot inlays, 22 frets, American Standard tremolo, locking tuners, and came with a certificate of authentication.

Fender Stratocaster American Standard

The early 1980s found Fender back in private ownership, wanting to create a new classic, and committed to making some Fenders in its new factory in Brea, California. By 1987 the American Standard was back in classic and updated style.

Music Man Silhouette

In 1986 Music Man unveiled the Silhouette, featuring such innovations as Teflon-coated truss rods with an easy-to-use adjustment wheel, and quick-change, solderless pickup assemblies. Also new was the 4+2 tuning key headstock arrangement. The Silhouette has proven a solid workhorse for such players as Keith Richards and Ron Wood.

Parker Fly

After more than a decade of experimentation by luthier Ken Parker, founder of Parker Guitars, and electronics genius Larry Fishman, the Parker Fly was launched in 1992. Parker had designed what is probably the most innovative guitar since the Stratocaster, incorporating a number of new technological and manufacturing patents into a beautifully streamlined package. The slender body is made of poplar, with a neck of lightweight basswood joined seamlessly to the body. The neck is reinforced with a coating of carbon and glass fibre. The combination of this carbon/glass finish and seamless neck joint give the guitar a superb action with seemingly endless sustain. The frets, unlike on most guitars, are made from stainless steel, more resistant to wear than traditional nickel/steel fretwire. The Fly has two humbucker pickups, to get a sound rather like a Les Paul, but they can be split for a warmer chord sound. The aluminium bridge has six Fishman piezo pickups set into it, for access to a full range of electric tones and an amplified acoustic guitar simulation. The Fly features a built-in preamp system, allowing you to play either the humbuckers, the piezos, or both at the same time. Players such as The Edge, Keith Richards and Joni Mitchell have used this guitar.

Vox Mk VI

One British company to achieve some measure of success against the American manufacturers during the 1960s was Vox. One of the classic guitar models that the company produced was the teardrop-shaped Mk VI. This most unusual looking instrument featured a bolt-on maple neck, three single-coil pickups controlled by a five-way switch, and a vibrato unit. The Mk VI shot to prominence when Rolling Stones guitarist Brian Jones played a rare, white, two pickup version on The Ed Sullivan Show. Although it was never a huge seller, sales increased steadily, and interest among players grew. The original 1960s guitars are now sought after by collectors.

Burns Hank Marvin

Jim Burns started his company in 1959, and by the mid-1960s his organization had become the most successful guitar-making outfit in Britain. In the 1960s owning a Burns was really something. Fenders were expensive and difficult to get hold of, and for a short time Burns was a force to be reckoned with. Top of the range was the Marvin, with its custom vibrato system, the Rez-o-tube, in which the strings passed through the body in pipes specially tuned according to the resonance of each string. The unit boasted 34 moving parts, and had the Hank Marvin signature etched into its body. It looked a bit like a Strat but with a headstock scroll design similar to a violin. The Marvin is the most sought-after Burns guitar, and as only 350 were ever made, demand for them is high. For a while the Shadows used nothing but Burns guitars and Vox amps. Bruce Welch's Marvin was made with a slightly narrower neck. In 1965 Burns was bought out by the American company, Baldwin.

Burns Bison

For collectors, the Bison is the next most desirable Burns guitar after the Hank Marvin. They hold a very strong appeal for many of the older British guitarists, who may have started their playing careers on them. The controls were volume, tone, two-way circuit selector and four-way pickup selector offering bass, treble, 'Wild Dog' and 'Split Sound'. The usual finish was black but some were produced in red.

PRS Custom 24

Paul Reed Smith is one of the world's premier luthiers and the founder and owner of PRS Guitars. Smith made his first guitar while at college and in 1975 set up a workshop at his parents' home in Maryland. Before long he was taking his creations backstage at concerts, convincing legendary musicians like Carlos Santana and Ted Nugent to try them. By 1982, Smith, having studied the traditional principles of Fender and Gibson guitars, arrived at his now famous, modern design. The Custom 24 is the core of the PRS line. The body is crafted from mahogany, with a maple top on some models. Necks are usually mahogany, although some models feature maple or Indian or Brazilian rosewood. PRS's signature fretmarkers are moons at the lower end, and birds at the high end. A five-way pickup selector includes coil-tap positions, converting the guitar's humbuckers to single-coil. Pickups are designed and wound in-house, and PRS is very secretive about magnet and wire type, and construction. Finishes are superb. PRS is known for 'popping the grain' on its figured, maple-topped instruments, a process that accents the 3D quality of the maple through a multi-step staining process.

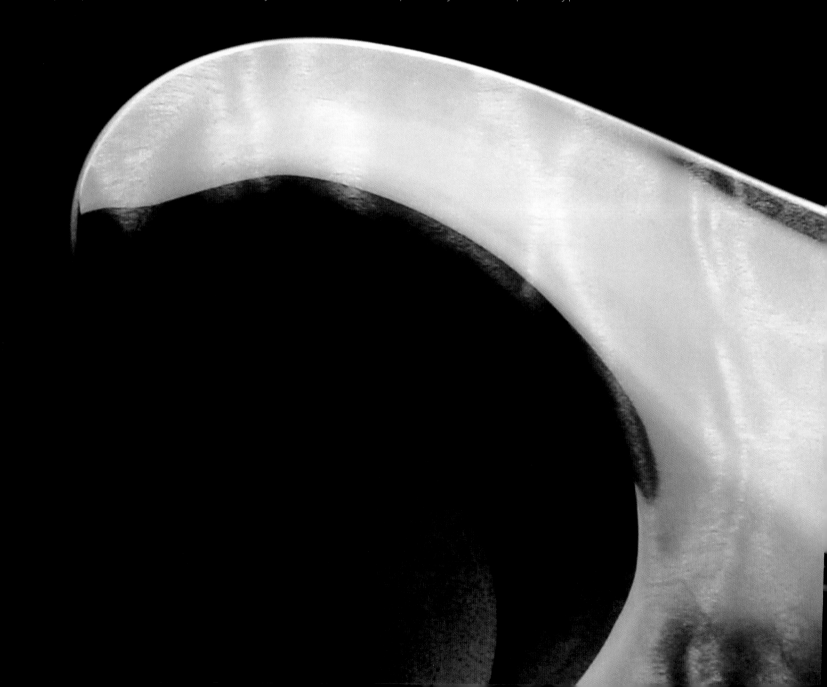

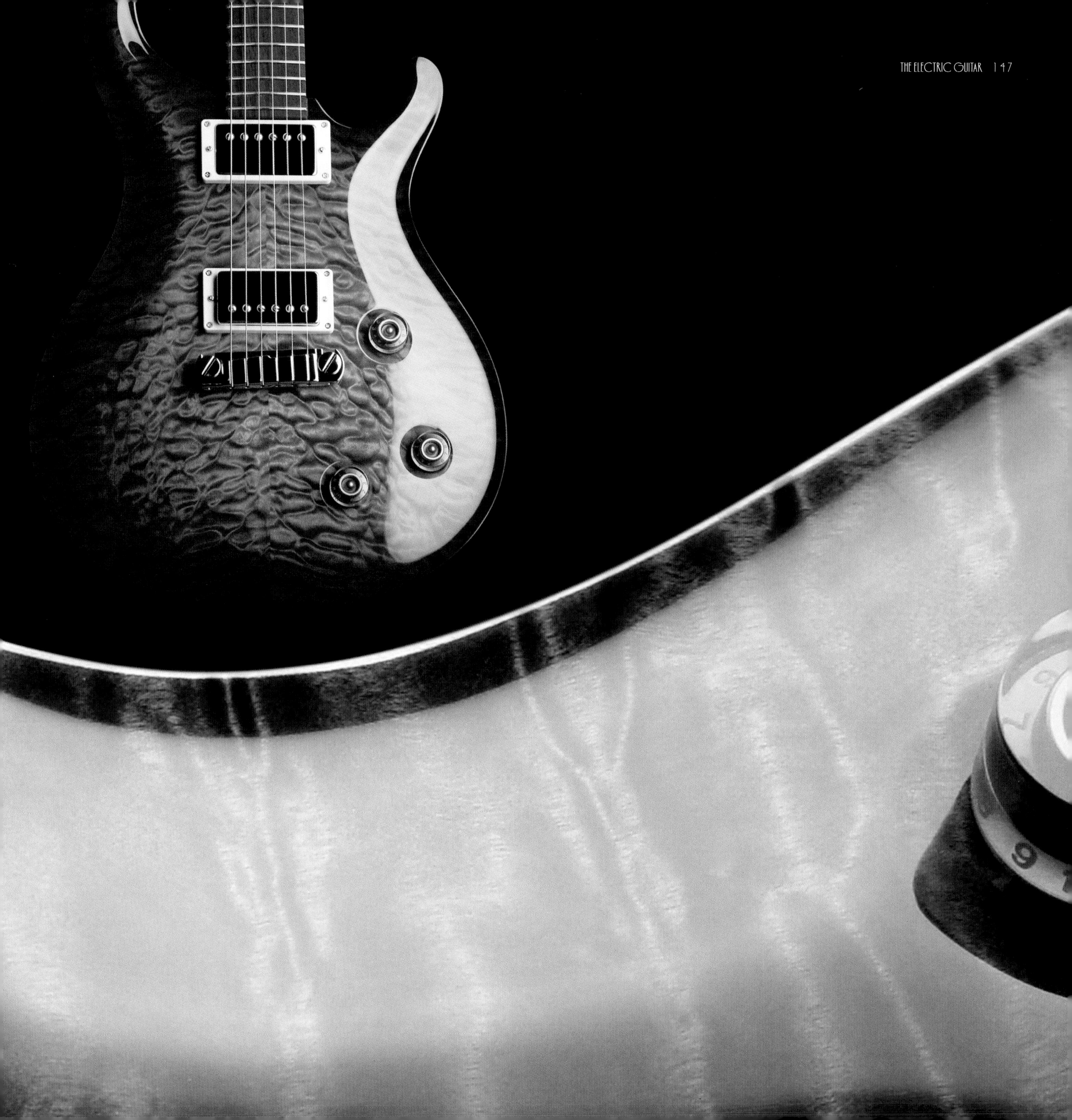

PRS McCarty Soapbar

This PRS guitar features a pair of soapbar single-coil pickups specially designed and voiced by Seymour Duncan, from a specification of the PRS Research and Development department. These pickups produce sparkling definition, with masses of punch. The maple top, thick mahogany back and stoptail bridge provide warmth and sustain. The instrument comes in a staggering array of colours.

PRS 2000 Dragon Series

It took many years of fine guitar making before Paul Reed Smith produced an instrument with a dragon inlaid along the neck. The first PRS Dragon was introduced in 1992, and with its beautifully figured top and exquisite inlay, it set a new standard for collectable guitars. It was also the first PRS with a 22-fret fingerboard. There have been four dragon models, each more exotic than its predecessor, the last of which – the 2000 – has more than 75 per cent of the body covered with 242 pieces of mastodon ivory, rhodonite, agoya, coral, onyx, sugilite, chrysacola, red, green and pink abalone, and paua bird inlays. Only 50 of these fabled 2000 series were made. They have maple tops, mahogany backs, Brazilian rosewood neck and fingerboards, with no fretboard inlay, two PRS Dragon 2000 pickups, McCarty-style electronics, stop tailpiece and gold hardware. Each guitar comes in a leather presentation case, with a certificate of authenticity. They are priced at around $30,000.

PRS Santana 2

Carlos Santana was a recipient of Paul Reed Smith's early instruments. He used them on stage and loved them. Santana's unusual 24-fret, 24-in (61-cm) scale signature model was one of PRS's earliest signature makes. He uses a Santana 2 guitar with PRS Santana 3 pickups without covers, and a tremolo, with .09–.42-in (.23–1.07-mm) gauge strings. Santana's guitar necks and fretboards are constructed out of a single piece of solid Brazilian rosewood, instead of the usual mahogany neck/rosewood fingerboard found on stock Santana models. The Brazilian rosewood helps create the smooth, singing, glass-like tone that he is famous for.

PRS Standard 24

The Standard 24 is designed around the original PRS guitars. The mahogany body allows access to the upper frets. The neck is mahogany and offers a 10-in (25.4-cm) radius rosewood fretboard that gives guitarists a wide yet thin neck. The chrome tremolo is matched with chrome low-mass locking tuners. Hardware includes HFS bridge humbucker, Vintage Bass neck humbucker and coil-tapping five-way rotary selector.

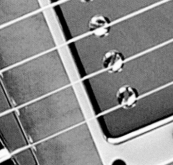

PRS Singlecut

Recently discontinued, the Singlecut had a carved maple top, mahogany back, wide mahogany neck with a 25-in (63.5-cm) scale length, abalone bird inlays, PRS-7 bass and PRS-7 treble pickups, volume and push/pull tone control with a three-way toggle pickup selector.

PRS Hollowbody 1

Lightweight and hand-carved, with only a small block under the bridge connecting the back and top, the Hollowbody has good acoustic qualities for a thinline hollow electric. The PRS Hollowbody archtop combines classic tone, comfort and understated beauty with a spruce top, fully carved mahogany back and sides and optional bird inlay. Other fetaures include McCarty Archtop pickups, wide-fat neck carve and PRS patented stoptail piece.

Gretsch 6129 Silver Jet

Gretsch launched their Jet series of guitars in 1955. The Silver Jet and Sparkle Jet were basically fancy versions of the black DuoJet model. With a Les Paul-shaped body the Silver Jet competed directly with the Gibson original. The body was 13 in (33 cm) wide, with a maple top, and two DeArmond Dynasonic pickups. Gretsch used drum-casing material for the sparkle, gluing it to the maple top. Double cutaways replaced the single cutaway style in 1961. Production of the guitar ceased in 1966.

Charvel Spectrum

Charvel Guitars were founded by Wayne Charvel in Azusa, California, and were made famous by rock guitarist Eddie Van Halen. In November 1978, Charvel sold his company to Grover Jackson, who in 1989 sold it to Japanese manufacturer AMIC. Charvel guitars were made exclusively in Japan to a very high standard. The Spectrum model was inspired by a custom Jackson guitar built for Jeff Beck. This unusual instrument was based on a Stratocaster, but with a reverse headstock, a Fender Precision Bass-style scratchplate, wild colours and an active tone circuit.

Framus Nashville

Framus was a German guitar, bass and banjo manufacturing company, which existed from 1946 until going bankrupt in 1975. The Nashville was well built but extremely heavy, with master volume control, master tone control, and a six-position rotary switch. A clean sound, with lots of sustain, but not a pretty instrument. A sort of Gretsch on a budget.

Hagstrom P46

Hagstrom, a Swedish musical instrument maker, started making
electric guitars during the 1960s. Many contemporary artists such as
Elvis Presley, Frank Zappa and Bill Nelson used Hagstroms. Most notably
today, Nicholas McCarthy from Glaswegian band Franz Ferdinand plays a
sparkle red P46. The P46 was the first solid electric guitar from Hagstrom. Two-
pickup and four-pickup versions were available, in various colourful plastic
finishes. Production ended for Swedish-made Hagstroms in 1983.

Aria Urchin Deluxe

The Aria company introduced the Urchin under the Aria brand name in 1977.
Built in the Matsumoku factory, the odd-shaped guitar did not catch on and
sales were poor compared to the company's more traditional instruments.

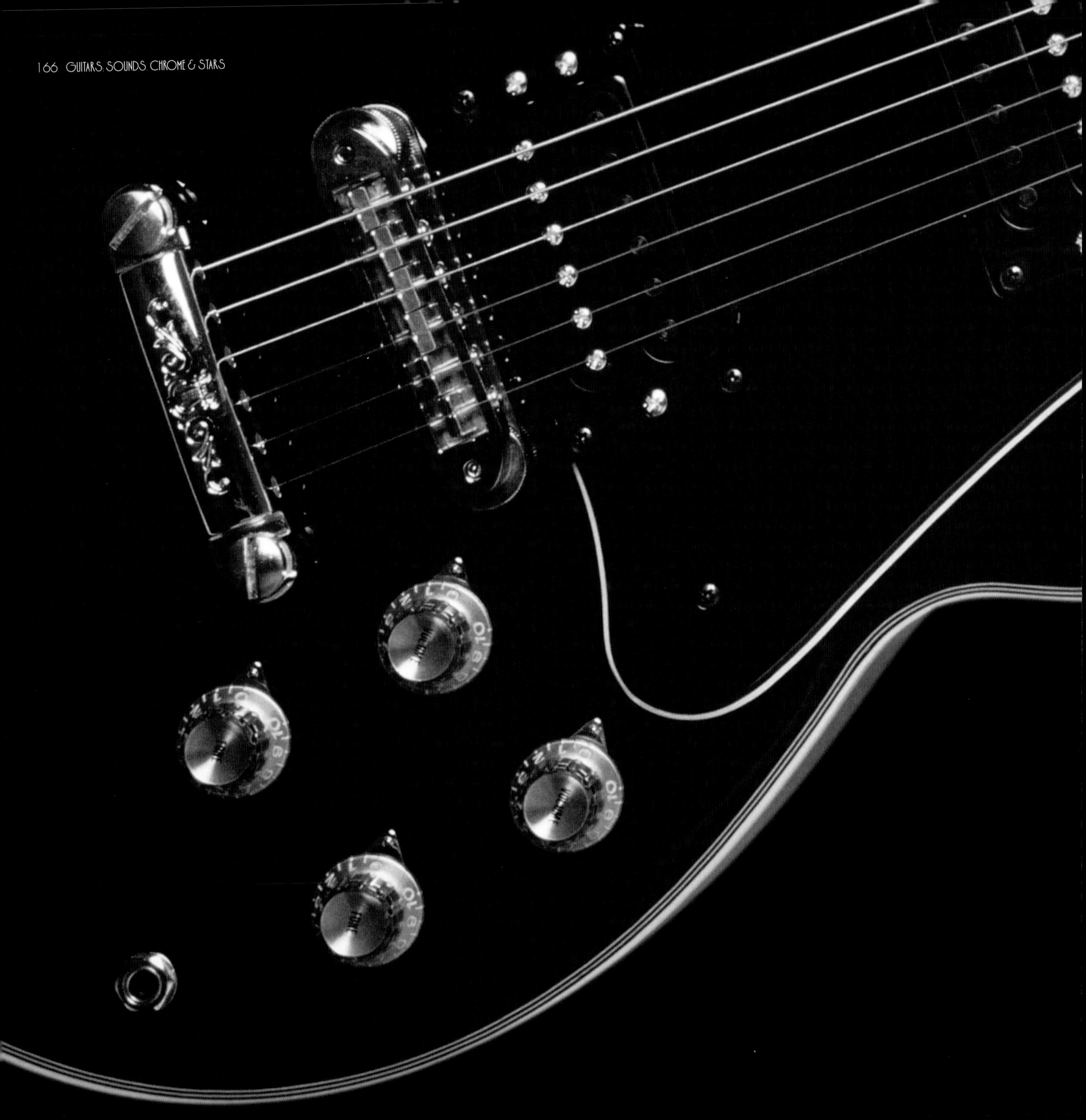

Yamaha SG2000

One of the great guitars from Yamaha, the SG2000 has reached almost legendary status. More than any other, this is the guitar that convinced players that the Japanese could produce an instrument to compare with the best in the world. In 1976 Yamaha introduced the SG2000, with a carved, solid, mildly figured, three-piece maple top, a three-piece mahogany/maple/mahogany neck-through design, a 22-fret, ebony fingerboard with mother-of-pearl inlays, twin Alnico V humbuckers and gold-plated hardware. A choice of five finishes was available.

Yamaha Pacifica

The Pacifica represents a fine introduction to the electric guitar. With its competitive price tag, it is considered slightly better than the Squier Strat, the standard beginner's guitar. It comes in a variety of colours, has one tone dial, one volume dial and is available in left- or right-handed models.

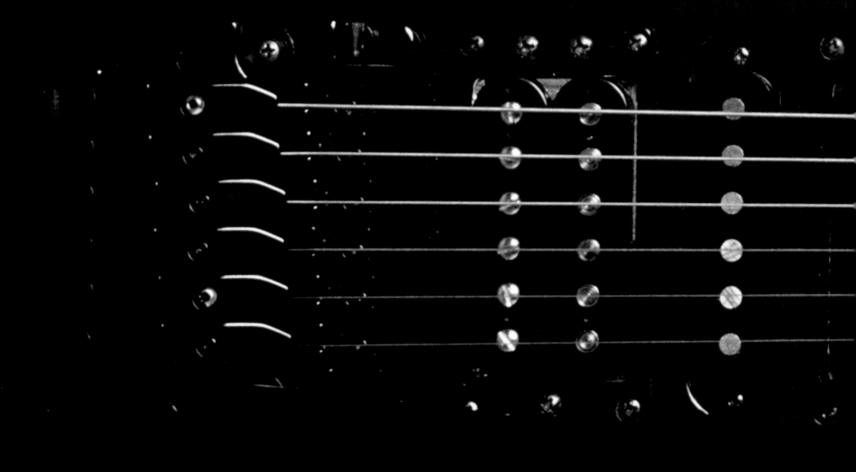

Yamaha RGX Custom

All Yamaha's guitar production is from the company's own specially built factory in Taiwan. The superstrat-style RGX Custom appealed to players looking for playability and aesthetic beauty. RGX models are still in production.

Jackson Soloist

The first official Soloist was serial no. J0158, completed in August 1984. The original models had standard neck through the body, 24 frets, ebony fretboard, 'sharkfin' pearl inlays and binding on fretboard and headstock. Pickup options were vast. A customer could get any configuration and any brand. Graphic finishes were practically unlimited, with custom colour or designs available for a surcharge. Domestic headstock logos will have 'Made in USA' below or alongside the 'Jackson' logo.

THE TWIN-NECK ELECTRIC GUITAR

Gibson EDS-1275

The Gibson EDS-1275 is a double-neck guitar introduced in 1958 as a special-order instrument. The original models produced between 1958 and 1962 were basically twin-necked hollowbody instruments with dual cutaways similar to the ES-175. In 1962 the EDS-1275 was changed to a solid-body guitar resembling the SG; this version of the double neck is the most common and best known among players and collectors. The guitar features two volume and two tone control knobs, a three-way pickup selector switch, and a three-way neck selector switch. It has single-ply white binding to the necks, vintage tulip tuners, parallelogram inlays and a black pickguard. The pickups are two 490R Alnico magnet humbuckers on the 12-string, and two 490T Alnico magnet humbuckers on the 6-string. The body is mahogany, with a maple neck and rosewood fingerboard. The model was popularized by Jimmy Page of Led Zeppelin, who used it when playing live performances of 'Stairway to Heaven'.

Gibson Double 12

In May 1958, franchised dealers were able to obtain the first electric double neck guitars ever produced on a commercial basis: the Gibson Double 12. They had one-piece mahogany necks with adjustable truss rods and rosewood fingerboards. The bodies, derived from the ES-175, were 17 in (43.2 cm) wide and 1 7/8 in (4.8 cm) thick, with a spruce top and maple back and sides. There were two humbuckers per neck, and the controls consisted of volume, tone and a three-way select for each neck, plus a master neck-selector above the 12-string bridge. The guitar was only in production from 1958 until 1962, and during that time only 46 examples were shipped. The price in 1958 was $475.

Gibson EBSF-1250 Double Bass

In 1962 Gibson introduced the EBSF-1250 double neck bass/guitar, a combination of a Gibson SG six-string guitar, and an EB-3 electric bass. It had a mahogany body, rosewood fingerboards and a built-in fuzztone which could be used for the bass and guitar necks. The bass section had two EB-3 pickups, and the guitar had two humbucker pickups. They were available in cherry, sunburst, white and black finishes. Only made until 1970, these Gibsons are extremely rare, with only about 30 having been made.

THE BASS GUITAR

Fender Precision Bass

Having created and marketed the first solid-body electric guitar, Leo Fender and his colleagues came up with another new and interesting idea: the electric bass. Introduced in 1951, the Fender Precision Bass was the world's first mass-produced and commercially successful fretted electric bass guitar. Prior to the Precision bass, players had to use the bulky, cumbersome, and almost inaudible double-bass, a fretless instrument that required a masterful technique to be played in tune. The Fender Precision Bass was usually made from either alder or ash, with a maple neck, and maple or rosewood fingerboard. From 1951 to 1957, one single coil was used, and from 1957 to the present, one split pickup, the pieces connected in humbucker mode. The P-Bass, as it is known, has a round, crisp tone in all its registers, perfect for complementing the other instruments in a rock 'n' roll band.

Fender Jazz Bass

The second bass guitar created by Leo Fender, the Jazz Bass of 1961 had a more articulate sound than the Precision Bass. The sound is richer and brighter in the mid-range, with less emphasis on the fundamental harmonic. Because of this, many players who want to be more 'forward' in the mix (e.g. in smaller bands/jazz bands), prefer the Jazz. It differed from the Precision with a neck tapering heavily towards the nut, and two separate pickups, giving a deeper sound.

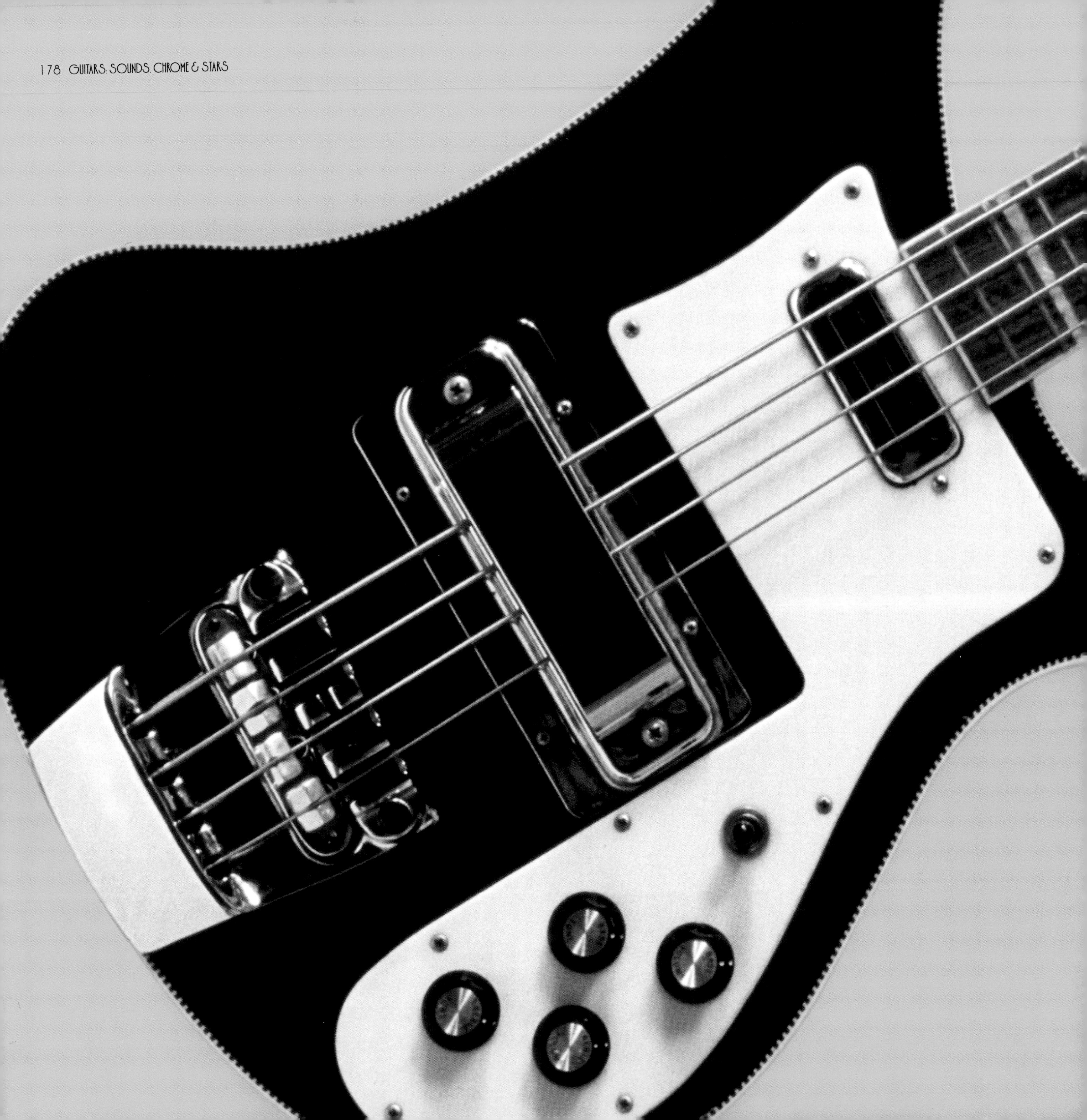

Rickenbacker 4001

The 4000 series were the first Rickenbacker bass guitars, in production from 1954. The Californian company's offering to bass players was as characteristic as any of its distinctive six-string range, with a long-horned body, curvy headstock and a neck-through construction that gave a more solid sustain due to more rigidity. The simple, single-pickup, two-control 4000 lasted until 1984 but by far the most popular version was the twin-pickup 4001 that first appeared in 1961. Early Rickenbacker bass users have included Paul McCartney, John Entwistle, Peter Quaife of the Kinks, and Roger Waters of Pink Floyd.

Gibson Thunderbird

The Gibson Thunderbird was introduced in 1963. Gibson had never been as successful with their bass guitars as Fender who, with the mighty Precision Bass, were all-conquering. The Thunderbird, like the Rickenbacker 4000, had a neck-through construction, where the neck wood went through the entire length of the body, with the rest of the body glued into place. It had a 34-in (86.4-cm) scale, equal to that of the Fender bass guitars. In 1966, Gibson changed the design. The original guitars had a 'reverse' or 'turned-up' headstock. In order to make the Thunderbird look more acceptable, Gibson flipped the headstock to a more Fender-like 'non-reverse'.

Hofner 500/1 Violin Bass

The 'Beatle' bass. Of all the fantastic instruments that the Beatles used during their eight years together, arguably none is more recognizable than the small Hofner 500/1 bass that Paul McCartney used. As McCartney apparently could not afford a Fender bass, he chose the less expensive Hofner, which he bought from Hamburg's Steinway shop in 1961. With a symmetrically shaped body, the instrument looked perfectly normal when played upside down by left-handed Paul. It was made with a hollow spruce/maple body with a short-scale (30 in/76.2 cm) rosewood fretboard. Controls were two on–off switches, two volumes and a master boost. These guitars produced a warm, rich, round tone.

Steinberger Headless Bass

In 1979 Ned Steinberger, a former industrial engineer and employee of Spector, a New York bass-making firm, designed the award-winning L2, a one-piece headless bass made entirely of carbon-graphite composite. It had no headstock for tuning, instead there was a redesigned tailpiece using micrometer-style tuners, and special strings with a ball at each end. The all-synthetic construction gave a very smooth sound and feel, immediate note attack, and even tonal response. Some players thought the sound was synthetic or unnatural. Another Steinberger innovation was the Trans Trem, a transposing assembly that detuned the strings in parallel so that the entire tuning of the guitar could be changed immediately. In the late 1980s Steinberger was bought by Gibson, who continue to make the models.

Ken Smith BT Custom Five

Ken Smith has been making basses for over twenty years, and has done much to popularize the idea of five and six-string instruments. He introduced the wide-neck six-string bass in 1981, and the wide-neck five-string bass in 1983, designed the compact quick-release bridge in 1983, and the replacement bass/treble circuit in 1986. All wood selection and final set-up are still done by Ken. Some of the exotic woods used include bubinga, lacewood, purpleheart and zebrawood. The hardware includes master volume, pickup balance, active treble, active bass and active mid-range.

Washburn AB 40

Launched in 1989, the AB40 is a cutaway acoustic bass with an arch top and back. It has a spruce top, maple back and sides, rosewood fingerboard and bridge, a bridge-mounted piezo-electric pickup, volume, bass and treble controls, and gold plated tuners. Washburn described the soundholes as 'acoustically placed sound slots', saying that they accentuate frequencies to give a warm, woody tone. These bass guitars are known for this rich tone, along with comfortable playability.

Westone Thunder 1 A Bass

The Thunder Bass was a very successful, medium-priced bass guitar from the Japanese Matsumoko company, whose other brand names included Aria, Epiphone and Vantage. The Thunder was usually made from maple for the body, with a rosewood fretboard with dot inlays and a volume and a tone control each for active and passive modes.

DIGITAL SYNTH & MIDI GUITARS

The use of special effects for the guitar became increasingly popular during the 1960s. These came through separate foot-operated pedals, offering tone-boosts, distortion and 'wah-wah'. A few manufacturers began building the effects into the guitars themselves. Traditionally synthesizers had a keyboard interface, but because synthesizers generate sound electronically, a guitar-synth interface provided an instrument familiar to a guitarist. The player could produce keyboard sounds from a guitar. Early guitar-organs were very unreliable, and also extremely heavy because manufacturers were packing all the electronics into the body. Roland solved this with a two-piece outfit consisting of a guitar and a separate synth box. MIDI (Musical Instrument Digital Interface) is an industry-standard electronic communications protocol that enables electronic musical instruments, computers etc. to communicate and synchronize with each other. MIDI- equipped guitars can, therefore, use the sounds from suitable synthesizers when connected to them via a MIDI. The latest development from Gibson is the HD.6X-Pro Guitar Sytem, allowing the guitar to be plugged into a computer via an ethernet connector, giving a staggering number of distortion-free effects straight to a mixing desk.

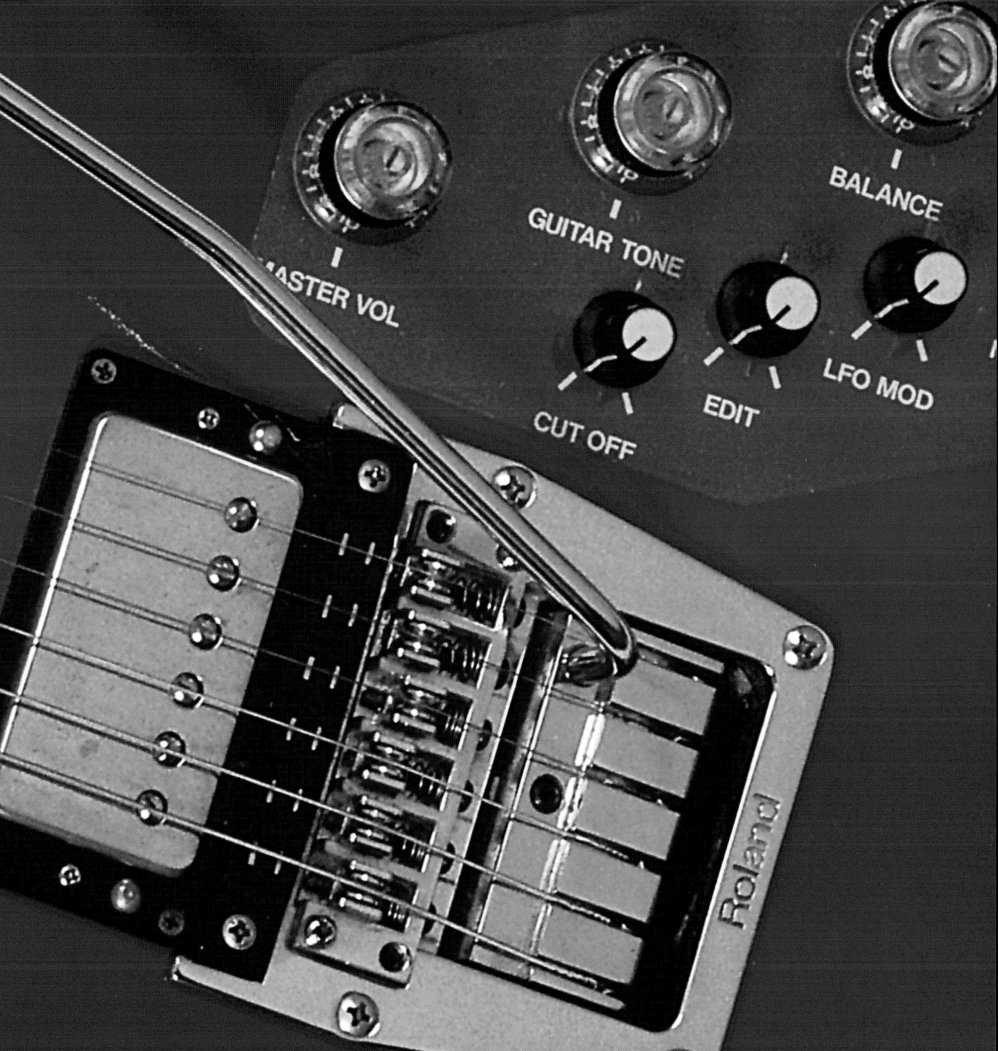

Roland G707 and GR700 Synthesizer

This unusual-looking machine was the third and last of Roland's guitar synthesizers.
Introduced in 1984, the G707 had an alder body, rosewood fingerboard, maple neck,
with a newly developed stabilizer, which eliminated unwanted neck vibrations, and
two humbucker pickups. The price (£2200 on launch), the odd shape, and the fact
that guitarists had no choice but to use the instrument with the supplied Roland
synthesizer technology, contributed to the guitar's lack of popularity. Production lasted
for about a year.

Vox Guitar Organ

In 1966 Vox introduced the revolutionary but problematic Guitar Organ,
a Phantom VI guitar with internal organ electrics. The instrument's
trigger mechanism required a specially wired plectrum that
completed circuit connections to each fret, resulting in a very
wide and unwieldy neck. The instrument never became
popular, but it was a precursor to the modern
guitar synthesizer.

Yamaha G10 MIDI

Yamaha entered into the synthesizer market in 1988 with a guitar-like MIDI controller called the G10. It was considerably less expensive than the Bill Aitken designed SynthAxe of 1986, which cost £10,000, though still out of reach for many musicians. The G10 featured two assignable knobs, and had six strings, all of the same gauge, which sensed both right and left-hand input.

Optek Fretlight.

The Optek Fretlight guitar got its start when Rusty
Shaffer, founder of Optek Music, was attempting to learn
electric six-string guitar solos. What he designed was a
guitar, based on a Fender, that showed where to put the fingers
to play a particular note, scale, chord or song, by using tiny red LEDs
in the fretboard. The Fretlight is computer driven and is controlled by
software from a PC via a USB cable. The software programme bundled with
the guitar teaches over 3000 chords, 500 scales, 550 arpeggios and notes on the
fretboard. The Fretlight can be used as a fully functioning electric guitar.

Roland GS 500 Guitar Synth

Roland made their name with keyboard synthesizers and sound boxes as a
premier manufacturer of sampled sound. They transferred their expertise into this
1974 unit whcih utilizes an Ibanez guitar body packed with digital modifications
(to replace the traditional electronics) and which plugged in, via a unique cable
conection system, to a sound-generating, synthesizing module. Sounds could
be mixed by using the complex knobs on the guitar itself, creating an incredible
range of soundscapes, from the orchestral, to the downright spooky. From the
guitarist's point-of-view, it can also make a good claim to achieving that rare goal
of never-ending sustain.

INDEX